Praise for *Healing Ourselves Whole*

"Emily Francis's book says it all. I had to learn as a surgeon about the power of the mind and how the body believes what the mind conceives. The truth is that we heal ourselves. When people have an unexpected recovery, doctors call it a spontaneous remission, but as Emily reveals it is not spontaneous but self-induced. We all have the potential to achieve that with correct coaching and our showing up for practice. Read this excellent healing manual and begin the process of becoming whole and complete."

—**Bernie Siegel, MD,** author of *Love, Medicine and Miracles*

"In *Healing Ourselves Whole,* Emily Francis connects the dots between thoughts and feelings—particularly the most deep-seated ones—and the body's physical response. This heartfelt book is a must-read for anyone struggling to free themselves from years of negative emotions so that happiness, joy, and health can become a daily truth. Emily holds your hand like a trusted friend throughout the process, encouraging you to journal, meditate, and go deep into yourself to release the emotional chains once and for all and to achieve healing on its deepest level."

—**Dr. Debbie Palmer,** author of *Mindful Beauty*

"Placing the tools and strategies for self-healing directly in readers' hands, Emily offers clear, experiential wisdom honed from years of personal work and study. As a yoga therapist, I often look for resources that will empower my clients and I will be recommending this, my favorite of all her books! This universally applicable volume of healing protocols will take any who use it into optimal wellbeing."

—**Jennie Lee,** author of *Spark Change, True Yoga,* and *Breathing Love*

"This book will take you beyond the symptoms into the root cause of physical and emotional imbalances. It is a perfect blend of Eastern and Western ideas spun into tangible steps so that readers can feel held, supported, and empowered by the process. This book is ideal for professionals and individuals looking to tap into the wisdom of their own bodies. It serves as an incredible resource for healing and feeling whole again."

—**Sherianna Boyle,** author of *Emotional Detox for Anxiety*

"Much like the jocular sage of Tibetan Buddhism, Emily disguises profound wisdom in a light-hearted tour of her own experiences as a bodyworker and healer. Yet, this is a book for the ages and, perhaps, for the sages too. In it are all the tools of the greatest healers: the wisdom of cause and effect, the magic of therapeutic metaphor, the curative intent of the most powerful shaman. Emily brings to conscious expression the causes and the cure and carries us along with her. Hers is an exquisitely sensitive prescription for a process of helping and healing that eventuates in a whole, happy and self-determined human being."

—**Steve Bierman, MD,** author of *HEALING—Beyond Pills & Potions*

"In her inspiring book, Emily Francis shares the culmination of her life's work thus far so we can become liberated through her unique tracking system. Under her powerful guidance, you will become fluent in the language of your body so you can deeply know who you joyfully and healthfully are. Thank you, Emily Francis, for this gift."

—**Bridgit Dengel Gaspard, LCSW,** author of *The Final 8th: Enlist Your Inner Selves to Accomplish Your Goals*

An Interactive Guide to Release Pain and Trauma by Utilizing the Wisdom of the Body

Emily A. Francis

Health Communications, Inc.
Boca Raton, Florida

www.hcibooks.com

Library of Congress Cataloging-in-Publication Data
is available through the Library of Congress

ISBN-13: 978-0-7573-2377-5 (Paperback)
ISBN-10: 0-7573-2377-4 (Paperback)
ISBN-13: 978-0-7573-2378-2 (ePub)
ISBN-10: 0-7573-2378-2 (ePub)

The material in this book is intended for education. It is not meant to take the place of diagnosis and treatment by a qualified medical practitioner or therapist. No expressed or implied guarantee of the effects of the use of the recommendations can be given or liability taken.

Publisher: Health Communications, Inc.
1700 NW 2nd Avenue
Boca Raton, FL 33432-1653

Cover and interior design by Larissa Hise Henoch
Interior formatting by Lawna Patterson Oldfield

Dedication

To all who choose to live our lives on purpose.
May we all find the courage, inner strength,
and peace of mind to live boldly.
And to my new home on the island of Malta.
Through the process of writing this book, I embraced
the opportunity to leave the yard.
Finally, and most importantly, I dedicate all the work I
ever do to my beautiful children and incredible husband.
It always comes down to you.

Contents

Section III: The Fabulous Four

Acknowledgments

Thank you to Steve Harris, my literary agent, for widening the sky's limits with opportunity.

To Camilla Michael, my editor, for making this book the most enjoyable experience and for the incredible support and expertise she gave to this work.

To everyone at HCI, my sincere thanks and gratitude for making this book a beautiful reality.

Overview

What Qualifies Me to Write This Book?

I'm not a doctor or a counselor. I'm not a psychologist or a psychotherapist. I am a bodyworker. When I use the term *body work* in my personal practice, I define it as an all-encompassing clinical approach to helping the body remember how to heal from within through hands-on applications such as massage therapy, neuromuscular therapy, and lymphatic drainage as well as energy practice.

Very few vocations in the world allow people to place their hands directly on someone to help heal, recover, release, and balance them. Body work to me is a sacred practice in which people entrust themselves to me during the time we have scheduled together. To receive body work, people must allow themselves to be quite vulnerable because, during a massage, they are basically undressed and draped accordingly. I, in turn, have the responsibility to create a safe space, enforce proper boundaries, and have a loving touch with no intention other than helping people to release and balance themselves. I do not take any sort of responsibility for someone else's healing; it is their own, and I honor that and support them through whatever they are facing. People do not come to me for a simple massage to relax. That is not what I do. I am both clinical and energetic in nature, and my approach comes with a specialized set of skills for people who are facing the aftermath of various traumas, most notably during or following cancer treatment.

I have developed a unique perspective on how our bodies store and release effects of traumas, pains, and shames. The body speaks to me, and I have learned how to understand its language. I can't fully explain it, but something happens when I put my hands on other people. Information is downloaded into me. I can almost hear and feel what their bodies are telling me.

The body is full of so much magic and wisdom, yet we have spent decades ignoring it in pursuit of other avenues by which to recover and heal. This book offers the truths that I have come to understand through my years of hands-on work and intuitive gifts. The other part of my knowledge of healing has come from a messy, sometimes debilitating amount of personal work to help myself heal from severe anxiety and panic. For a long time, I struggled to regain control over my health and happiness. When I say struggled, I mean I went all the way down with it. This was not a little blip in the story of my life. And just a few years later, I had to use what I learned about the various aspects of body healing and apply it to my child, who has functioning recovery, and the removal of her diagnosis of an autism spectrum disorder. People hear our story and think it's not possible, but I say to myself, to my children, and to you: *No one has any right to tell you what can and cannot be done in the name of healing.* All things are possible, and miracles do happen. It's a matter of gathering information from far and wide, committing ourselves to a life well healed, and keeping a strong faith that the only limits are the ones we accept.

The Body Charts

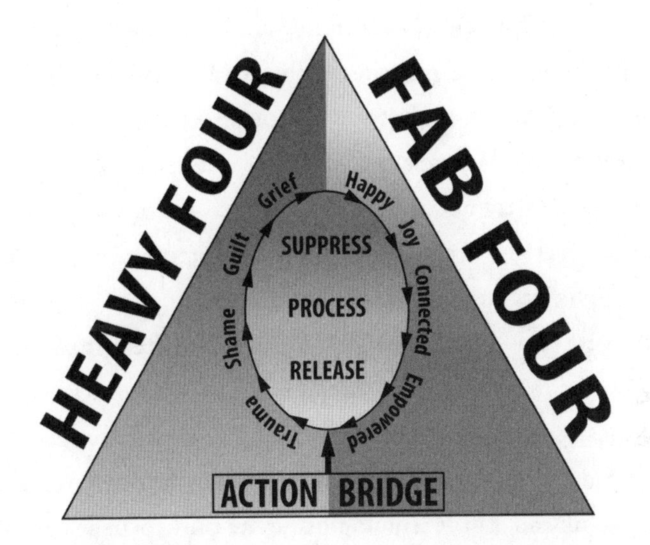

Teaching you how to rearrange the dialogue within the body is my primary goal for writing this book. I am someone who has theories on just about everything. I also tend to notice little details that most people miss both in regular spaces as well as when it comes to anyone's body and behaviors. I have spent years dialoguing with various bodies and gathering research from far and wide. I have homed in on the way our bodies store memories, as well as the way bodies communicate what they are holding. I have created two charts from all my studies: the *muscle emotion chart*, which is located in the back of the book, and the *somatic emotion chart*, pictured above. The muscle emotion chart illustrates where we hold emotional pain and why.

When we suffer from chronic pain in a particular area but nothing has been able to help, we must then look inside and figure out the emotional piece of that puzzle. It is the act of understanding and liberating the heavy body pain. The other chart, the somatic emotion chart (*somatic* is a fancy term for *body*) summarizes how I find the body to store emotional experiences and how we can work through them for release and renewal. Both charts are based on over twenty years studying these subjects. I consider them my life's work. These charts show how I have come to know and understand the messages of the body, and use these messages to teach us all how to take control of our own healing once and for all. Now we can use these practices to champion our cause for improving the health of our minds and bodies instead of perpetuating self-destruction.

Working through each aspect of the somatic chart can liberate each of us in an entirely new way. What I'm starting to learn is that using these charts does more than help us recover from traumatic events and PTSD. That seems to always be the big focus on healing, and rightfully so, but it should not be the only focus if we want to truly heal. Our life is not a summary of a few tragedies. It is a compilation of all our experiences. Those situations create a pattern for each of us, which evolves into how we process everything that comes at us. Without realizing it, we begin to lace those behaviors throughout our entire system. How we feel and internalize each individual situation in our life is not an isolated situation at all. It's a pattern that we've set up and continue to act from until work such as this provides us the opportunity to reevaluate what we have anchored to us and from there begin to make new choices. My hope in offering this interactive book is that all the tools you will need for this work are provided within this text. You will find journal prompts in each chapter as well as a guided meditation, which you can listen to on my website, www.emilyafrancisbooks.com. Click on the audio tab, fill out the information, and we will email you the audio meditations.

The Theme of This Book

The theme of this book is working with our bodies' emotions and memory systems to help us heal. This work does not replace the potential need for medication (there is no shame in that game) or other counseling methods (which I highly recommend). This book provides the work of the body and of your connection with your body for the purpose of unity and health. Using the somatic chart, we start from the heavy side of emotions that I dub the heavy four: trauma, shame, guilt, and grief. Then we will learn to cross the action bridge from suppress, process, and release into living with the fabulous four: happy, joy, connected, and empowered. If you follow each of the chapters, write in your journal faithfully, and listen to the audio meditations repeatedly, I can promise you that the power to heal and shift will become totally yours.

The Setup for This Book

Every chapter in this book will follow the same basic protocol. Each chapter will focus on one of the various body emotions stored within us. The way we will approach the healing work will be quite uniform. Through meditation, we will follow the process in which we learn to identify various issues held within the body. We will learn to get grounded in our body and to identify where the roots of various pains were planted within us. From there, we will follow the process of pulling the embedded memory from our soft tissues, which I refer to as *carrots*. We will remove one carrot at a time and fill the empty space with something loving and nourishing (remove and replace). Following the meditation, each chapter will have journal prompts for you to document your information as well as a paired affirmation with a hand-to-body position, or mudra, in order to solidify the work that you accomplish before you move to the next section of somatic memories. You can also find printable copies of the journal prompts on my website if you need more space for writing or do not want to write in the book. They are located under the Journal tab.

In the action bridge portion, we will incorporate actions beyond the remove and replace method. We will first learn what suppressing emotions does so we can decide to move beyond keeping it all down as we allow the memories to percolate and rise to the surface in the processing section. Following the processing part, we will practice a release technique through cord-cutting. The remaining sections of the book will cover the high side of emotions and body memory for health and healing, known as the fabulous four. These are happy, joy, connected, and empowered. For work with the fabulous four positive body emotions we will not remove, replace, or release. We will instead keep in place the carrots that have blossomed and pick from those blossoms to plant more carrots to multiply strong and healthy experiences throughout the body's memory tracks. It will require a lot of effort on your part, but it will be worth it.

Introduction

You Are Not in Pieces

Many times, we find ourselves in a battle between who we once were, who we are currently, and who we'd like to become. Often we are an embodied case of shredded thoughts and feelings that have not yet found their way into becoming a seamless tapestry that makes up the whole. We remain stagnant or may feel broken for so many reasons: behaviors such as self-talk, wicked fears of a million things, self-doubts, thoughts and feelings never expressed, traumas never brought to the surface and healed, guilt and shame patterns that run so deep that nothing could ever formulate from that space. There is no fixed, simple way to turn all the broken pieces into one healed whole. There is, however, a part of the deep shadow healing work that has been greatly overlooked until now, and I believe this is the reason why so many people feel like they "did the work" and did not obtain the desired results. For way too long, we have been working from the space of just our thoughts and behaviors. The truth is that the body holds the experiences of your life just as heavily as the thoughts do. Although different than repressed thoughts that often happen, the body does not ignore these repressed experiences as long. What does not get acknowledged will show itself through physical pains and health issues. Therefore, when you do the release work through cognitive efforts as well as learn to tap into your body and release these experiences through the body, this is the game changer.

Even if you feel broken, the truth is that you are whole. Every piece of yourself that you feel might have been lost is salvageable. It's all in there, but it needs to be created anew into something much better than it was to begin with. It's not putting pieces back; it's taking items that have been stuck in time, attached to various traumas, and bringing them into the present in order for you to heal from all of it. It's learning how to listen to your body's stories and how to work with your body as a team in your healing. It's offering the opportunity for the mind to process any grief, shame, trauma, fear, or guilt and then to turn the entire system into a balanced, healthy, calmer, and lighter system. It's releasing the old and creating something better with it. It's learning to understand the way both the body and the mind individually handle our emotions and traumas. One cannot truly work without the other. They are the yin and yang of any healing process. One is dark; the other is light. One is day; the other is night. One is the shadow, and the other is the light. You cannot have one without the other, and the body and mind are no exception.

Kintsugi

When a ceramic bowl, teapot, or vase breaks into tiny pieces, most would throw all the pieces away. However, in the Japanese tradition of *kintsugi*, they believe in repairing the broken pieces by joining the fragments together with gold sealant. They believe that the breaks and repairs should be highlighted as the piece now comes together in a new way, and the fillings bring the piece together into an even more refined look than its original shape. Each fragment is now joined back in a new way, and every repaired bowl, teapot, or vase now looks different and unique. It does not have a single identical match. The breaks in the piece now highlight and enhance its unique beauty. They believe the scars are what makes the piece more beautiful. This is known as *kintsugi* (金継ぎ), or *kintsukuroi,* (金繕い), literally golden ("kin") and repair ("tsugi").[11]

Something to Note

Emotions are not words. *Feelings* can be put into words. *Emotions* are tied to the actual physiology of the body. We *express* our feelings; we *experience* our emotions. Emotions are created in the brain.[1] As a whole, we miss this incredibly valuable and real concept. Emotions encompass how we experience feelings, and this is a whole-body-system language. When looking into the emotion of anything in your life, you must learn how to track the physiology of the body's response with its pairing. The physiology is the part that sits within the body itself. We also need to learn how to move the body in different ways, as well as incorporate meditations, affirmations, and visualizations to create the most dynamic healing avenues possible. The process can be very messy, but the results from the work can create true and utter bliss in your life. As Cynthia Occelli says, "For a seed to achieve its greatest expression, it must come completely undone. The shell cracks, its insides come out and everything changes. To someone who doesn't understand growth, it would look like complete destruction."

Above all, you need to know that you are fully capable of learning how to flip the script with your internal dialogue for healing. You have within you the power to create a new reality within your body—both physiologically and psychologically. It will not come easily. You do have the power within you to make it happen, but you have to trust me on that until you can get to the point where you start to trust yourself.

Together, We Can Face Really Difficult Things

There are a lot of ways to say *you have to do the work and fix it yourself!* But if you aren't given the tools and maps that allow for this to happen, then we are all listening to the same self-help agendas with no firm solutions for how to get there. We've all done it. We've all listened to people who have clearly done their work tell others that it can only be done within yourself. I'm one of those people who always says that true and lasting healing only occurs within yourself, and I still stand by that. This part is true, but I've never expected you to do it by yourself. I've always said it is entirely possible to do, but it is virtually impossible to do alone. This book comes as my sincere offering to you as a guide into the drop-down of your secret self, where damage and destruction might still be buried beneath the rubble. I have a deep desire to offer you the help and support to mend all the broken pieces that no one has ever helped you to locate and love. Not every person can afford the type of extreme counseling and therapies that allow for this transition to occur. And many times, this extreme counseling is simply not enough to put it all back together. There is a part of healing that has been grossly overlooked, and this is precisely where my work comes in. What we need is the whole-body perspective to healing. Here is the big-ticket item that we have overlooked when it comes to healing in full: *The body must play a leading role in our healing process*. This cannot be a mind/memory-only process if we want to gain true and lasting results from the work we are about to put in. We know that muscle memory exists, but too many times we only associate it with memories for purposes of physical movement. The muscles themselves hold everything that has ever happened to us.

Muscles aren't the only storage units within the body, either. The fasciae that encase both the muscles and the vital organs are information highways for moving energy throughout the body. The fasciae are basically the highway systems (or channels) where the experiences of life have been downloaded and stored within the body itself. Meridian channels, used in Chinese medicine, run along the matrix of the fasciae, and each specific meridian channel details certain emotions. The cellular memory idea has floated around for decades; we understand that it exists, but we haven't used it well enough to offer the release work that this way of healing requires. As a whole, we need to learn how to use both the body and the mind to release stored pain, shame, trauma, guilt, and the memories that go with them. We also need to do better with remembering that we can tap into the same avenues—the muscles, the cells, the energy, the fasciae—to pull up the really amazing memories that we have stored within and use those to remember and create more fundamental joy and happiness within. There is substantial research around positive emotions correlating to improved overall health.

When I was in my own self-destructive phase of life with no clear purpose and no clue how to put myself together, I went on a quest for healing that has and will remain a lifetime pursuit of healing and balancing. I went to all sorts of expensive therapies even when I was broke, living on the pull-out couch at my mother's house and counting bodies for paying bills in my massage practice. I have been down in places so low that only those who are willing to admit to their failures and setbacks can understand. But you will find as you get more honest about who you really are that it's the messy, honest, and raw examples in your life that you will feel the most freedom from. We are about to embark on a very deep level of self-healing. I will guide you through every step of the way.

What Makes This Different from Other Self-Help Books?

I have read so many books on self-healing and attempted so many ways to pull myself up when I had exhausted all the options through all the various therapies. I have tangled with the likes of real-life wizards, energy healers, and shamans who did their very best to "heal" me. I have had soul retrieval as well as hypnotherapy, EMDR therapy, acceptance and commitment therapy, talk therapy, behavioral therapy, spiritual communication for therapeutic measures, and so much more. I've been everywhere I've ever heard of in my quest to become a functional member of this life. I have sought medication, herbal remedies, group sweat lodges, and meditations.

Through my own major work of learning how to heal from the deep, dark places that used to linger within, I have accumulated a lot of wise counsel from those who work day in and day out to help others do the same. I am a compilation of everyone I've ever worked with and everyone I've ever worked on. I, too, have helped a great many people come into new spaces within themselves that have allowed for huge shifts to take place in their lives. I have done the work required to claim peace and happiness within myself, and there was a long time when I never thought this could be possible for myself. For other people, sure, but for myself? Once upon a time, that did not seem possible.

Twenty years ago, my world was all about health and wellness and exercise. I was an aerobic director, kickboxing instructor, yoga instructor, and a health and PE teacher for a time before I went to massage school. However, I was always running away from how I really felt about myself deep down. In all honesty, I was also a heavy drinker at that time and had no idea just how deeply I was self-medicating to mask those feelings. I was totally wild as a teen and in my early twenties. I embraced the role of the party girl. I realized when I turned twenty-five years old that I was getting extremely close to the point of no return. I had arrived at the crossroads and I knew it. I made a crucial decision to stop drinking completely for one year. It was a commitment I made to myself to see if I could do it. This was the beginning of my daily and lifelong devotion to the work it takes to heal all the way through. It was extremely difficult to have all the things I had stuffed down and run away from come flying back up. I became someone who suffered so badly with anxiety and panic that I lost my footing with all the things I had been doing in my life. For years I had been the motivator, the cheerleader, the positive and bubbly happy girl, and I just had nothing left to give. Everything I had been stuffing down and never dealing with had all come to a head, and I went down hard. I got to a place where I barely left the house and left everything and everyone behind to wallow in my misery of being afraid of everything. I quit my job, I moved back home, and basically stopped talking to most friends. I did not know how to do the deep-dive work that was required to get my life back and make it better. That is when I started my writing. It just wasn't worth talking about it to people anymore because no one really could understand how I felt. It seemed like I was saying the same things over and over in trying to make anyone understand.

In hindsight, the conversations sounded like I was defending the pain and sorrow. It felt like I was out at sea with no life preserver in sight. I was drowning in every aspect of my life. My pad of paper became my closest confidant. It's not like I was a writer in school either. I earned Ds in English literature. I wasn't one for good grades until much later in life. I just knew how to party and put on a great show until one day I couldn't do it anymore. I always say, "One day the mask dropped, and the crazy appeared." No one helped me figure it out initially. When I first told someone I was writing a book, the response was, "Oh yeah, right." (This is part of the reason I always advocate not sharing your dreams with friends or family until you are making them into reality. We don't need those kinds of people pulling us back when we finally choose to create something new for ourselves.) I did all the work myself. I never stopped writing either. I have been writing this book for more than fifteen years. I never gave up on the work, and I never gave up on myself or the possibility of a better life. I had one area of expertise that I felt passionate about, and that was healing, which led to writing. It was the only thing I knew and loved. I have been faithful to these concepts, and they have been faithful to me. It is also the reason behind the journaling offered within each chapter. Writing down the experiences that you have through this work is important to document and confirm that what you are working through is shifting for the sake of your higher health and healing.

Once my year of no drinking was over, alcohol didn't have the same appeal to me that it once did. The attachment to it had been severed. But the work that I had to go through with the therapies and recovery from the emotional trauma of my life had only just begun. Removing the alcohol simply opened Pandora's box and I had to make the choice whether to face it all or run away still. I chose to do the work. I am now offering a level of that work to you through this book that was not offered to me. I had to figure out the body memory work for myself. Without including the body's memory patterns in our health and healing, I do not believe we can create the level of wellness that is possible.

I also must say that although I have done incredible work and have healed from my past up to the present, *this is life!* There will be more to come! And we will have to prove to ourselves again and again that we are worthy and deserving of vibrant health and a radiant life! We will most surely be presented with situations in which we will have to apply our new tools to heal ourselves again, just not from the same things as before (we hope). We are all a work in progress, and we will all find times when we fall. The trick is to be able to get up faster and get back to center more easily because now you know how to do it. By having the journals filled out, you can take yourself into any healing situation with a quicker response time, because you will know the ways that you respond best. By the end of this book, you will have faced all the dark and embraced your light, too. You will have new guidance on how to scan your body, listen better to its messages, and catch things much sooner, before they fester into something poisonous. My intention for us all through this work is to become more sensitive to our bodies' needs and tend to our gardens with a much softer hand.

Whatever you give your attention to, you will create the reality that matches it. We will learn to harness our thoughts in these pages, and more than that, we will learn to drop ourselves down into the rabbit hole and allow ourselves the time it takes to fully heal what's been keeping us tied down. If you are faithful to this work, you will create the opening for all the best things that life can offer. We in the self-help healing field often say, "You have to do the work to get the results you want." This book offers you the path to do the work so that you can achieve the results. If you commit to following each chapter and filling out the journals and listening to the meditations, as well as creating your personal affirmations and pairing them with your touch techniques as you repeat them, you will take yourself through the shadows of yourself and clean house from the inside out and the outside in. You will get to know your body and how it handles pain, as well as your mind and how it processes pain in a way that can result in real-deal outcomes.

I have wracked my brain to figure out how to help someone go down to the depths of despair and darkness to build the way back up to something new and desirable. How do I best share this process so it is meaningful enough to stick? I have helped countless people do this work and heal from very deep wounds, but it was always through my hands-on work. It's very difficult to find deep healing just through the process of reading a book. There are always incredible nuggets of wisdom in any book on healing, of course. But I wanted to offer this to you in a way that could make a big difference in your life. I have provided audio files to lead you through the meditation practices. It's difficult to read through them and then put the book down to practice. By pairing your journal writing and affirmations with your touch techniques, this book will truly offer you every tool you will need to work through your body memories on your own. The way that I would scan your body and figure out how to best treat it will now be offered to you in a way that allows you to learn to apply this to yourself. Through this work, you will learn to take your power back and harness it for the creation of the greatest good and highest joys for yourself.

My last two books, *The Body Heals Itself* and *Whole Body Healing,* offer a lot of information on why we carry pain where we do and how to go about finding the right team of helpers to truly heal ourselves and our lives. This book is different because it is just for you and you alone. No other healers to gather around. No other counsel. Just the work itself. We will dive deep into our bodies and understand how our bodies and minds store pain and how to gently escort that pain up and out safely and effectively. This will bring you through the shadow work that people talk about but are not very forthcoming about helping with. I have personally collected research for this book. Through my own process of healing, I have met with psychotherapists, spiritual counselors, psychologists, neuropsychologists, shamans, naturopaths, homeopaths, acupuncturists, other people who are lost and struggling, a multitude of bodyworkers and hands-on energy workers, and many more to fully put together deep and authentic offerings.

It was important for me to seek out advice and insight from the very best for you, but you are not required to go see anyone but the mirror with this work. It is entirely about you. I am here to walk you through the process, so you won't be alone facing this task. Facing the hardships that we tend to stuff down deep into our soul pockets requires bravery, and the willingness to get disgustingly honest with ourselves. Some of the hardest parts of this will be the willingness to get totally raw and naked and sit with the discomforts that are guaranteed to arise. I will help you through the discomforts as we travel all the way down and all the way back up to someplace new. I'm guiding you as your bodyworker, as well as a person who has truly done this work. I will be your tour guide and your friend throughout this work. I know what it's like to be stuck so far down and in so many fragments of thoughts and feelings that you can't see any way out. I am a woman who has released all my secrets, had those secrets thrown back in my face (this is always a possibility when we put ourselves out there), and created a life for myself that I am so very blessed to be living. I am still and will always be working on myself to maintain the balance that I've found. Or I will be working on myself when life kicks my ass (which it will) to rise up even higher than I have been before. I will also teach you how to stop and take stock of the changes that have been made and just how far you have come from the beginning of this journey. We must learn to become our own best advocates on our healing walk.

I used to think that the only people who got to live extraordinary lives were *other* people. But why not me? And why not you? The answer to the question of *why not us*? The answer: It *can* be us! And . . . it *will* be us! Here is another quickie but goodie: There is enough happiness, self-worth, and positive living to go around for all of us. Our becoming something wonderful does not in any way take away from anyone else's ability to be happy. I think many people somehow miss that little jewel. People fear that if we heal and become the best version of ourselves that it will somehow take away something from others. But this has nothing to do with the people around you, and we will need to navigate through this part as we make the changes necessary to reclaim our lives. We have all been granted the same human right to live however we truly want to live. We just haven't had the proper guidance to get there until right now.

Acute Versus Chronic Pain

Your body sends signals to you through the avenue of aches and pains. Aches and pains are a part of the human existence, and inevitably along the way, we are sure to experience such inconveniences and wave them off because we don't know how they got there or because we've lived with them for so long that they simply have become a part of us that we don't stop to question. Because we are disconnected from our physical bodies, too many times the signals that our bodies are sending us as a direct message get lost in translation. As schoolchildren, we are not taught about our physical bodies in a way that includes daily thoughts and behaviors. Things like "don't fall or you'll break your arm!" seem to be the most abundant forms of body conversations with our young people. We do not learn in school the value of deep breathing, coping skills, ways to calm ourselves by using the breath, or ways to taper our thoughts. We are not even taught much about the organs within our bodies and what they do! It easily happens, then, that unless you have veered off and started studying a practice or chosen a form of healthcare on your own, you might not know how to listen to the messages of the body. This way, those pains that occur without explanations simply become something of what is. *It is what it is* has become a common sentence that drives me crazy. It's never *what it is*. It is not something that you should just accept blindly without explanation. The body doesn't work that way. It doesn't come up with random pains or illnesses out of the blue. The body is a straight shooter when it communicates, but we are not straight receivers to its communication.

Let's imagine that we have a new pain occurring. This is known as an acute pain. It is recent. It is not embedded in the muscle body or the memory systems. An acute pain happens when we trip and fall, run into the table, or are involved in an accident. We can identify the source of the pain, and treating it can be fairly quick and straightforward. An emotional pain can be something acute, as in happened recently, but it is not like an acute physical pain. In general, emotional pains are from experiences that happened long enough ago that you may or may not have the line traced between its inception and the chronic pain that occurred from not treating all the aspects in a straightforward way. Traumas that occur both physically and emotionally do not come with a quick-fix guide. They are multilayered, and we must use great care and patience with these discomforts. It can be difficult to draw the line from inception of the pain to the current circumstance. It is not easy to detect the root causes of every pain that has burrowed into us. In many cases, due to the amount of time that has gone by since the infliction of the trauma, we can't imagine that our bodies have held on to things that happened in our youth or adolescence for so long.

Honestly, I find that the most vulnerable pain pockets in the body were planted during the most raw and formative years. It is now up to you to follow the meditations, find the pains and traumas that have been planted, and let them tell you their story. Not the other way around. For this, you are the observer. Once the information has been shared, then you will become the healer. Approach each of these situations with care.

No One Knows Your Story but You

Whether it is in articles or my other writings, I usually approach from the angle of support and comfort in knowing that you are not alone. However, here you are alone, in a way. That does not mean that you won't have support because you are always supported, both from here and from the heavens above, but this work is extremely private. When it comes to any life experiences and traumas that have planted themselves inside you, only you carry that story. Even the other people involved won't have the same story about it that you do. There is literally no other person in the entire world who will share the stories that you have about anything that has occurred in your life up to this point. That's exactly why learning how to work inside your body to help yourself heal is of the utmost importance. It is all about you. It's time to take your power back and use it for your greatest good and highest joy without guilt, without shame, and without reservation. It's also your story to tell whenever you are ready and wherever you choose.

When it comes to the way I lay out the meditation practices, they are uniform for a reason. Your trauma might be incredibly serious, and someone else's might not be considered as serious. The practice of learning to scan your body and listen to its messages of holding patterns is unique to you. The intensity level of your experiences is specific to you and your life. I strongly encourage you to allow your body to speak to you without any filter that you have unconsciously placed on it. Whatever messages, images, and stories that come up are from your memory vault within your body.

You Are Not Tethered

Have you ever passed by the houses where the people don't treat their animals with the love and care that those who treat their pets like family do? Have you driven by the dog that lives outside on a chain all its life? Whether it's raining or sleeting or snowing or storming, that poor dog is stuck outside. (It breaks me every time.) Or that live in those tiny little cages with their one little doghouse? Every day looks like the same thing. All they wait for is a meal and someone who will give them love. What a horrible way to live. I wish I could free them all and teach their owners how to treat animals. (Or if I'm being honest, I wish I could save all the animals and throw their owners in jail.)

Do these animals have any idea how life could be different if they lived in a different setting with different people? Do they know what life is like with love and affection? Do they have any idea that with the right support system and love, they could become therapy dogs or rescue workers, sniff out cancer, save lives, or be the greatest lap dog that ever was? If they were given the chance, would they run away? *Do you know this about yourself, too?* You can truly become anything you desire and show up for, but first you have to be open and willing to change the scene.

The Story of Belle

Everyone in animal rescue has that one animal that got them into it. For me, it was Belle. Belle lived outside her whole life. Every day, I took a walk with my dogs and our baby stroller. I always saw Belle lying on her back steps. I wondered all the time if she ever got to go inside. It turns out the answer to that question was no. Not ever. She lived outside day in and day out and ate rocks as her source of entertainment. One day her owner took off, moved away, and left her behind. I was afraid of that dog. She was a bully breed, and her bark was ferocious. She barked at us every time we walked by. She seemed so aggressive. I still really wanted to get her someplace safe. Her neighbors, of course, wanted to have her put down. I enlisted a more compassionate neighbor to help me, and we decided to split the vet bills and take her in to get checked. When we opened her gate and came in to see her, she let us love all over her. It turned out that she wasn't aggressive in the least! When we tried to get her to leave her yard, she would not go. Putting a leash on her and pulling her out of the fence was nearly impossible. Getting her to leave the parameters of the only life she'd ever known? Not possible! We could not get her in the car. She would lie down and refuse to move. The neighbor and I went home extremely disappointed that we couldn't get her to come with us.

But then a friend I knew very impersonally at the time, from Facebook no less, sent me a message and offered to come with me to pick up the dog and get her to the vet. I accepted her offer gladly. That next day she went up to the dog with no trepidation, scooped the dog right up in her arms, and placed her into her van. While we waited at the vet's office for the results of her tests, my friend looked me squarely in the eye and said, "I'm not taking her back there. I am hoping to set off a chain of events that leads to this dog getting the life that she deserves, and we are never taking her back to that place ever again." She put everything into motion that she intended to do from that first day. That dog ended up living in her "groom room" (she is a professional dog groomer) for longer than she anticipated. She had to help the dog feel safe and know love before she was ready to get out on her own with new people. We all need that down time to heal sometimes and learn there are better ways of living life. Finally, she found the perfect family. That dog lived the rest of her days knowing the most incredible love. She went to the park every single day for a walk. She had two parents who were retired and were with her all day long. This dog, our sweet Belle, changed all our lives forever.

I offer that story because that is the same plan of single-pointed focus that I have in mind for each of you. I hope through this work that we, too, will set off a chain of reactions that will allow you to realize that, unlike a dog that lives on a chain, you have free will and the full ability to change the yard you are currently living in. It doesn't mean you have to move, of course, but it does mean that you can unhook the tether, which will result in changes in your scenery. Like Belle, who was afraid to leave the only yard she'd ever known, we will likely run into that same feeling as we are faced with letting go of tragedy and pains that have implanted themselves into our bodies for so long that it can be incredibly difficult to feel okay without them. Together, we can set off the chain of events and reactions that allow you to create a version of yourself so you will never go back to that other place ever again once you learn how to remove and replace in your own gardens. When we go down deep within ourselves, face our shadow sides, and learn how to live from a space of balance, recovery, and peace, our whole lives will begin to shift and align beyond what we can currently imagine possible. If you are feeling anything like the dog I discussed, know that where you are today is absolutely no reflection on where you could possibly end up.

You Have Everything It Takes

Let me be clear: you are not *too old*, it is not *too late*, you did not miss your chance, and wildly exciting opportunities at life are absolutely possible and available for you. You can do great things even when you think you can't. It simply becomes a matter of how much you want it. It's the rule of three for life evaluation that one of my greatest spiritual teachers used to ask me: 1) Who are you? 2) What do you want? 3) What are you willing to do to get it? Once these are defined, the path becomes clear. Asking these three questions consistently throughout your life will help in enormous ways to keep you focused and on track to become who you want to be and reach the places where you really want to go. I have included these three questions in the following journal to help you get a laserlike focus on what you want out of this book and out of your life.

I will be here to guide you (and you can even reach out to me directly to help support your journey and I will write you back at www.emilyafrancisbooks.com), but as I've always said, it's still up to you to do the work and create yourself in the authentic image and life you desire. You can live whatever life you create from here, but it has to be real or you will continue to chase the ghosts of your life.

Let's unhook the chains that are making you feel tethered and go for a really well-deserved ride. May we all kick our skeletons out of the closet and dance with them. Let's bask in the sunshine of opportunity and self-love. Believe it or not . . . *you deserve to be free and happy*. Onward and upward we go . . . but first we have to drop all the way down. It will be okay. Let's do this.

JOURNAL

ONE Who are you? Not the superficial person that the outside world might see, but who are you really? What are you about? What do you stand for? This is more thought-provoking than it sounds. Get detailed when writing down what makes you tick and what things you like and dislike about yourself and the world you are living in. This includes what you will tolerate and what you won't. What are your deal breakers? The more you write, the more you circle back to a few key points that define who you are in this world. Without realizing it, you will also find insight into who you want to be.

____

____

____

____

____

TWO What do you want? This is *so* important. You must constantly come back to this one again and again to be aligned with what you really want in every aspect of your life.

____

____

____

____

____

THREE What are you willing to do to get it? This is the deal breaker question. You might want all kinds of things, but are you actually willing to do all the work it takes to make them happen? This defines what you really want in your imagination and what you really want in real life. There are lots of things I thought I wanted until I found out how much hard or boring or taxing work is required to actually get them. Only the strongest desires come with a willingness to do the work that is required to make them happen. Get into those, and then you can formulate a true plan to make them real.

___

___

___

___

___

Section 1

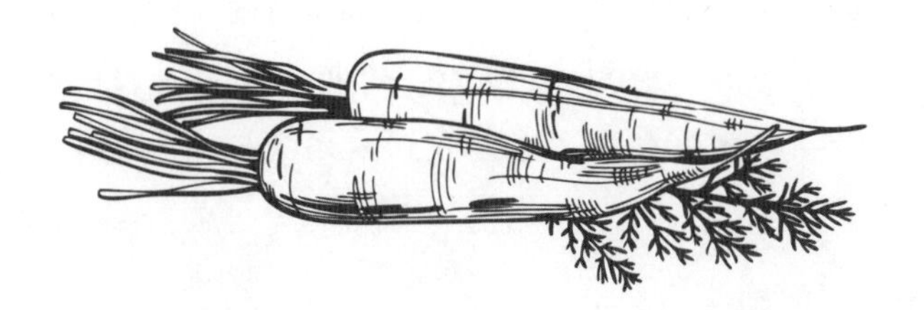

The Heavy Four

According to my research and findings, our bodies hold these emotions, the heavy four: 1) trauma, 2) shame, 3) guilt, and 4) grief. This cycle of trauma, shame, and guilt especially is the hallmark in the making of dis-ease. It's a never-ending cycle beginning with infliction and then being recycled over and over again to punish ourselves and keep us trapped in our own little hell based on these realities. Grief is different from the cycle of trauma, shame, and guilt, but it is anchored within every cell and tissue of the body in a devastating way that is not self-perpetuated the way the other cycle is. It just sinks down, and we are tasked with trying to live our lives with an incredibly deep cut producing an open wound that makes it almost impossible to breathe for a very long time following its infliction.

The Karate Kid

Allow me to offer a very simple story, but one that made me aware of how easy it is for the mind to change the narrative of any given experience. When I was ten years old, my neighbor, my mother, and I went to see *The Karate Kid* in the theater. It was, and remains to this day, one of my top movies of all time. I am so grateful that I got to see it in the theaters. When my dad got back from a business trip, I had him take me again so he could see it. That movie, in my memory, brings great delight. My walls were covered in magazine photos of Daniel Larusso (portrayed by the actor Ralph Macchio). My dad bought me the cassette tape of the movie's soundtrack, and I learned every word of every song.

Many years later, I read an interview with one of the supporting cast members discussing the cast's experience of making this small-budget movie, which they had no idea would leave such a lasting impression. He said they all went to see the movie on opening night. They sat all together in one row. At the end of the movie, people got up on their seats to clap and cheer. He said the whole theater was wildly celebrating, and the actors looked at one another with a sense of knowing that this held the possibility of being a hit.

Several years later, I finally showed my children the tournament scenes of the movie. I found myself telling them that I got to see this movie in the theater when it first came out. I then went on, without realizing that this story was actually not my own and told them that after the last scene people were climbing up on chairs and clapping and cheering. I had this incredible realization that I had merged someone else's story into my own. I can't actually remember if people clapped and cheered or stood on seats when I saw it in the theater. I have changed the narrative about how I envision the end of this movie. Now my interpretation of someone else's experience of the story has muddied what I can remember of my own experience. I realize this is not a big deal; it's a movie. However, it does show how easily our narratives within various experiences can converge into another scenario without our realizing it. Our minds are wide open to sensationalizing any event, whether it's something insignificant like a movie or something big like a tragedy.

The Animated Narrative

Different cultures have different belief systems to explain the various elements of the mind. This is what the Native Americans refer to as *coyote medicine*, or medicine of the mind. It's the trickster, and it loves to be animated and play tricks on you. The Buddhists refer to this as the *monkey mind*. Again, it is the animator of stories that like to confuse and excite the mind. This can happen to the stories that we associate with trauma and tragedy as well. When a trauma insults the physical body, many state that they eject themselves from their body in order to survive. The memory of the assault (be it physical, emotional, or sexual) usually pairs with a bit of haziness because we became so deeply disconnected from the body itself during that time. The body, however, was not given the opportunity to leave itself. It experienced all of it at the time of impact and beyond. The body does not align with monkeys or coyotes or any other storyteller that likes to play it up for the audience. Our bodies tell our story, and they tell it through the narration of straight-shooting truths. They sugarcoat absolutely nothing. Learning to listen to the message of our body can liberate us in a whole new way. Working with the body on the heavy emotions is the goal of this section.

The practice of these particular meditations involves using a *remove-and-replace* model for dealing with our trauma, shame, guilt, and grief. We will begin with relaxing our entire physical body, then deeper layers into the organ system, and then deeper into the soft tissues of the body. In the space of the soft tissues, there is a garden that holds deeply rooted carrots for each heavy experience that has planted itself into us during the course of our lives. We will only work with one carrot per practice. We are asked to sit with the carrot and allow it to tell us its story as the body experienced it, not with the accompanying narrative that the more audacious mind tends to describe. Once we have allowed the carrot of that emotion to share the imprint with us, we ask permission from our body to remove the carrot and replace the empty space with a quick-setting liquid to heal the space. Nothing good comes from leaving a wound open without treating it so it can heal. That is the practice of these four chapters.

Chapter 1

Trauma

Trauma is locked in the body, and it's in the body that it must be accessed and healed. Trauma responses are fundamentally highly activated, incomplete biological responses to threat, frozen in time. —Van der Kolk[2]

We begin with trauma because the understanding of trauma covers basically every life experience that produced a negative consequence that your body took on and stored. When it comes to the body, each experience gets tracked and from that moment begins a new system of communication, whether we are aware of it or not. Think of a tracking system not related to the body for a moment. A tracking system observes and analyzes what occurs within someone or something. A tracking system is a monitoring system compiling data based on a sequence of events. There is a timing to the events that stack up on one another from the moment the tracking begins. The sequence of events becomes the underlying detail in tracking anything. Now think of the body, and imagine that we have several tracking systems that run throughout it. I refer to them as *body memory systems*, but it is the same exact thing. A traumatic event in your life can put a halt on one or more of the tracks that the body uses to communicate. When a true trauma occurs, the brain (which is an organ) releases the chemicals that make the body physically react. The brain, along with the spine, makes up what is known as the central nervous system. It has communication tracks within the nerves that receive and transport messages throughout the body. The central nervous system is how we understand and activate the fight, flight, or freeze responses. The nerves transmit messages to the muscles to react based on the sensory input from outside sources that signaled to the brain that we are under threat.

The mind (where thoughts and behaviors live) and the body itself lock into their specific tracking lines from the moment the impact/trauma occurs and remain that way until specific assistance is applied to help free up the tracks of that particular situation. Trauma by definition *results from an event, series of events, or set of circumstances that an individual experiences as physically or emotionally harmful or threatening and that can have lasting adverse effects on the individual's functioning physical, social, and emotional well-being.*[3] Trauma may come in one of three ways. First is acute trauma, which is something that is a single occurrence. Once is definitely enough where trauma is concerned. Second is chronic trauma, which is something repeated, such as physical, sexual, or domestic violence. Lastly, complex trauma is an exposure to multiple events. This usually occurs during wars.[4] According to the *DSM-5* definition, it requires "actual or threatened death, serious injury, or sexual violence... Stressful events not involving an immediate threat to life or physical injury such as psychosocial stressors... (e.g., divorce or job loss) are not considered trauma in this definition."[5]

For the record, I disagree with these criteria. For anyone who has suffered through a divorce or the effects of a divorce, that trauma is extremely real. Veterans who experience combat are more than likely to experience complex trauma and are diagnosed with PTSD (post-traumatic stress disorder). However, PTSD does not occur solely in veterans. Anyone can have PTSD from a traumatic event where they just can't seem to get past it. I was diagnosed with PTSD many years after losing my father suddenly. The doctor said that even though I had done tremendous work around my healing, I still had PTSD and it was still frozen into my thirteen-year-old self. It is so much more common than we once understood. I think most people who experienced a significant trauma will have PTSD because it insinuates that the trauma is sticking close to you. In a way, PTSD has become a catch-all term.

Unintentional Trauma

Let's talk about trauma as something that insults all your senses and changes the way your body responds to certain stimulus from that point onward but was never intended to cause you harm. Childbirth could be considered a trauma. I know firsthand that having a C-section (although it was executed beautifully and basically flawlessly twice) was an assault on my body even though the intent was not to inflict pain or damage. My body will never be the same as it was before I had children. Many women have extremely traumatic birth experiences, and their bodies will never have the same memory tracks that they had before a child grew inside, kicking its way around, rearranging almost all the organs, and then following an exit plan that, either way it goes, all but desecrates the pathway out. Not everything that changes us was meant to harm us, but the events rearrange our internal systems nonetheless. These are no less serious or intense. These are still traumas. We just approach them slightly differently. Our bodies signal that deep pain has occurred, and our bodies still have those messages to share with us. Other people may have had a lifesaving surgery, or been intubated, or battled serious illness or addictions. Those are all traumas. From that point forward, whatever part of the body that was affected may carry phantom pain that can only decrease but never fully release its hold. When we discuss trauma, it is all-encompassing. Therefore we must treat ourselves with delicate hands in our recovery.

When we consider complex traumas and repeat traumas that offer a deeper dialogue concerning the types of trauma people endure, these topics, too, require a different approach and level of awareness. Understanding the complexity of a trauma gives us a stronger platform from which to dive. It's the same thing as *getting to the root of the issue,* a topic people so often discuss when healing is involved. That catch term used to be focused on getting to the root of our pain or suffering. However, just learning what type of trauma we have or what the actual root of something is only offers information. It doesn't actually change anything. It's what you do with that information that matters. It's the platform from which you can begin your journey. That's it, nothing more and nothing less than gathering basic solid information.

Trauma, once inflicted, tracks deep into both the psyche and the body. It's a point of impact to both the body and the mind. It inflicts damage to the entirety of the body's memory systems. It affects the entire sensory system. It is important to understand that the traumas in our lives can create a pain pattern from the moment of impact and that the pattern remains in place until we learn to remove it or at least to rearrange it so it doesn't hold us so tightly.

Traumas that are frozen in time do not mature with age. Even as we mature, we continue to view specific traumas through the eyes of whatever age we were when they happened. From there, they play on a repeat reel. There is something about experiencing trauma that I don't feel enough people understand: The mind has an ability to check out in many situations when trauma is involved. Some refer to it as shock. After an accident, more times than not the person will be hazy about the experience and cannot properly recall the entire set of events. We go into shock so that our minds can shut down and we don't have to be in our bodies during the actual experience.

Many victims say that when they were being physically or sexually assaulted, they ejected themselves from their bodies and hovered above so that they would not have to feel all of it. That is a gift of the mind that helps us to survive the experience. People talk about looking closely at the ceiling, counting cracks in the wall, or doing anything with their thoughts that allowed escape from what was being done to them. The body, however, does not have that same luxury. The body cannot leave itself. With that being said, in situations when people experience extreme fear, the body will release hormones that will lessen the mind's perception of actual pain, but that does not erase the experience from the body.[6] The body takes the pain and absorbs the trauma. Those memories of experience remain that way. This is why hypnotherapy as well as EMDR (eye movement desensitization and reprocessing) therapy in particular can help people to pull the memory of a trauma through the deep subconscious and then learn to bring the memory into real time and out of the frozen time track where the mind has it stored. When we learn how to add in the piece of the actual body trauma and how to help our body release the stored pain and trauma, then some of the bigger magic can happen. While I cannot offer you hypnotherapy or EMDR therapy (although I highly suggest them), I can help you work through your body so that you can release the emotional hold.

The Approach into Healing

How we approach the processing part of the healing work varies widely among trained professionals. For a cognitive therapist, this work would be approached in the way that we *think* about each trauma. The work would concentrate on how we understand it and release it. In my work, I concentrate on the body itself as the primary vehicle to *feel* and process pain. We will learn how to transmute our pain into something more useful to restore our bodies to something closer to their original state. Any significant and traumatic impact crashes itself into our bodies and embeds into all the systems: the muscles, the fasciae, the organs, the cognitive mental memories—everywhere within the body. Of course, traumas are also held hostage within the mind and the mental memories. I believe that we have spent decades of healing trying to get our minds to access the body in order to heal the body when, in many cases, if we access the body itself for healing, the mind goes right along and allows for a more thorough approach into full-body release and repair.

When any significant impact occurs, it remains exactly as it entered into the system and stays that way until we do this work. This is why it is referred to as being *frozen in time*. The memories that keep the trauma alive do not change over time without assistance. They don't figure out a way to heal or to mature without our full understanding and cooperation to bring them into real time. Therefore, our expression of the pain manifests itself in many different ways through 1) our behavior and 2) the pains or body issues that we carry. The behavior aspect is more of a cognitive approach. This requires a trained psychologist, psychotherapist, or someone of that nature who works primarily with behavior patterns and mental aspects to understand the issues and help people process their griefs and traumas. The body healing is done through people like me and other professional bodyworkers who work with the neuromuscular system and the energy lines within the body.

Creating a process where the body and the mind agree on the story allows it to be accepted as it actually happened, instead of as the narration you created around it. Once the story is brought up and seen as it actually happened, we can start the process of seeing it from a more honest perspective and therefore removing the extra burdens around it (your specific attachments to it). The body always holds the memory as a straight situation without any dialogue added around it. It holds the facts. The mind holds the facts with its own opinions and feelings around it. It also tends to change the narration to something we can handle. Until we do work such as this to lift it from a cycle of repeated experience, pull it into real time, and digest it from our current level of awareness, it's nearly impossible to finally process and release it once and for all.

I have found that the muscles hold emotional traumas, pains, shames, and grief as well as the good things: joy, bliss, and other delightful emotions. This is all part of muscle memory. It's all in there. The experiences of life are embedded in the muscles themselves. Joints, however, do not actually store those things as the muscles do. The joints tend to tell your story in real time. When our joints flare up, it's not always because we are getting old. It might be because we are experiencing symptoms such as feeling overwhelmed or stuck and not nourishing ourselves mentally and emotionally. If our joints are always in pain, that can certainly be a direct result of putting on extra weight, both physically and emotionally, but I do not believe that the joints are holding stations for past traumas. Certainly they do not hold trauma the way that the soft tissues of the body do.

In Chinese medicine, it is believed that memory is transported through our body via the blood and plasma. Our cartilage has memory.[7] Most notably, the cartilage of the nose has extremely prominent memory,[8] yet it does not have blood flow! Our bodies have all sorts of memory systems. Some memory areas (like cartilage) govern what their function should be. Other soft tissues within the body are able to trigger the memory connections from sensory input such as sight, taste, touch, smell, and sound and from the energy that surrounds something that happened previously, either positive or trauma-based. Nothing in the body operates independently. The intertwinings of the various tissues all play more than a singular functional role within the system. This is why we need to approach the body without singling anything out and while allowing the body itself to guide you on how to work with it to heal.

In both my experience and research, joints tend to show exactly where you are currently. What I am about to introduce for the joints is the emotional component. This has nothing to do with issues such as osteo- or rheumatoid arthritis, as well as physical damage to any joint. For example, when our knees begin to have issues without an injury, more often than not it's a direct result of not making a decision on an issue that is weighing heavily on us. We are standing at a fork in the road and feeling stuck, as if we are in quicksand and just can't seem to make a move in one direction or another. Our knees signal that we are stuck, so they may swell or feel achy. It's a communication tactic of the body that few know how to decipher in a timely manner. When we finally make a move and notice the pain gently fades away, we chalk it up to a simple coincidence, if even that. When pain goes away, it's amazing how quickly we forget about it and never track it to something real or emotional happening in our lives. The ankles tend to demonstrate the sweetness of life. Therefore, when we deny ourselves the love, happiness, and decadence that we can have, our ankles start to act up. Again, we can be so quick to dismiss this connection that it goes unnoticed. The body often communicates our emotions through swelling, aches, and pains. Strains and sprains, however, are a direct result of an actual injury; those are not the same as an ache or a swelling without a traceable cause. Bruises are a direct result of an actual physical force that impacted the body. A bruise does not randomly come up without a cause-and-effect occurrence. Nothing comes up in the body without a cause and effect, but bruises show themselves much more easily due to the discoloration that occurs following the impact. With joints, it can also be easier to read what is happening in our lives because generally they are very cause-and-effect in nature. You can draw the lines.

The hips are gatherers of information, and they are the direction seekers. The hips point to where we want to go, but if we don't move toward that direction, a disconnect can occur on an emotional level. The shoulders, elbows, and wrists match the hips, knees, and ankles directly as well. The shoulders embrace or repel life situations. The elbows govern our ability to redirect and follow through. The wrists support. If any one of those joints randomly swells, it is always worthwhile to do a body scan and check yourself mentally to see where you are currently in your life. Do you feel overwhelmed and don't know what your next move is? Feeling under pressure, as if the weight of the world is on your shoulders? This may result in chronic tension in the tops of the shoulders and trapezius muscles. These are all things to start noticing and practice dialoguing with yourself.

The muscles are harder to track because they hold emotions that have been put into their storage units at any time throughout their lives. These stored emotions may not be discovered until you actually go through this work and make some connections into them that you haven't yet made. As you follow the guidance and begin to scan your muscles for undetected carrots that have been planted throughout your life, please know that I am asking you to be more honest with yourself than you may have ever been. Reserve judgment about the things you think *should* be there and concentrate instead on what actually *is* there. Your body's story is, in general, markedly different from the story of your mind. The story you keep telling yourself might not be the story your body experienced. It is important to be reminded of this as we go along, for best results. As you begin to work through your body for healing, remember that we are creating a no-judgment zone. That is why I offer the opportunity to write journals in here. It's your own work between your physical self, your conscious self, and your deeply hidden self. It's time to become a unified front made out of total realness and interconnection that can only be created through dropping down into the rabbit hole and changing up the script to something freer within ourselves. Your journal entries do not need to be shown or shared with anyone else. They are private work that you do with your body for your own healing.

Pain Is Not Random

Pain can be a blanket term for discomfort within the body's physical and emotional structure, but it is rarely, if ever, random. A bruise from bumping into a corner of something can be considered random (although some might argue this point). Pain, however, is a message. Pain is a language of the body.

The following explanation of the body occurred while I was treating someone dear to me for whiplash after she was in a serious car accident. I knew by her voice that she had experienced a decent amount of whiplash because her voice was crackly and weak. I went to her house and set up the table. I helped with the whiplash by treating a lesser-known muscle that requires me to gently move the trachea over and treat the part of the spine in the neck from the front of the body due to the force that pushed that muscle forward on impact. When I was finished, she had her voice back. When I had my hands on her, I could feel this push-pull happening between my hands and her body. I realized in that moment that because it was so close to the actual time of the trauma, I was able to help the body dialogue what had occurred. I could not in any way reverse or even distract from what had occurred. I could almost feel the processing of the accident trickling into the tissue memory beneath my hands. Her body was trying to process what had occurred in real time, and I was trying to cause a distraction and help reverse some of the pain that was going to come with it.

I realized then that even when we can intervene quickly after a trauma, the trauma is still going to penetrate all the soft tissues and get into those memory tracks. It happened. We can't take it away. We can lessen the depth to which it will be planted inside us, but we cannot remove it completely. I could not intervene and change how her body experienced the actual crash. I could, however, help to dialogue with her body to support it during its time of processing to help release a lot of the physical pain that accompanied the crash itself. I could also offer support in the way that the muscles would carry the pain by manually releasing the areas that were tensing up the most. It's amazing what the body can tell you if you know how to work with it directly. I could put together a lot of information that she had not thought of by knowing what muscles were locked up. Through the muscular pain patterns, I could actually put together the way her head was facing at the time of the impact. I had questions for her that she hadn't had time to think about yet. The questions I was asking her were not questions she would ever go back and ask herself. It would only be at a massage therapist's office, chiropractor's office, or physical therapist's clinic that she would be asked the kinds of questions I did in order to get a better idea for a treatment plan. It made me realize that we can do a tremendous amount of healing on every level, but the healing practices, no matter which kind, will never take the trauma away—not completely, anyway. What can happen, however, is that the healing can help to rearrange the dialogue that we have in relation to the experience itself, and that is the big-ticket item in our ability to heal well.

By doing this work through our physical bodies in relation to trauma of any kind, we can change the way that we understand it and the depth at which we hold it. However, we are foolish if we think that we can erase it. I think this is exactly why my friend and spiritual counselor who works in addiction medicine always says, when it comes to a place of forgiveness, that the acceptance of all situations "as they actually happened" is paramount in moving beyond them. We must always begin in the place of the reality of any given situation that caused us pain. We must be willing to accept the situation as it actually occurred and without the extra storytelling that we naturally tend to extend to it. No one means to change the narrative, but it's a very human response. Listening to the body and not just the mental narrative allows us to find the original reality without change in the accuracy of the situation.

Pain Pockets

The body stores pain in various places as a way to hide the pains from the seeker. I refer to it as the *apothecary method*. When I work with a body and come across an area that is holding on to trauma or pain, it will stuff that pain into another place within the body, hoping not to be discovered. It is a natural response to the discovery of hidden pain. I think of them as little soul drawers or pockets, just as an apothecary has so many different drawers. When we get to an area that is vulnerable to the physical or emotional trauma pain roots, it will go into a fear response of freeze, flee, or drop. The body is in no rush to discover the roots of pain and remove them. As with any behaviors that we become addicted to, we have no idea how to live without them, even if those behaviors and thoughts are completely destructive. Becoming naked and removing the roots feels like one of the most vulnerable experiences. It can be extremely overwhelming, and we must fill those empty spaces quickly if we are to do this right.

While we have trigger point charts, somatic emotion charts, muscle body charts, meridian channels, and the organ correlations for emotions, this does not necessarily dictate where your pain is being stored, nor does it decide what that particular emotion is to you. We all have our own pain pockets, and they can sit within your body without a particular rhyme or reason. While all of these charts provide incredibly useful and valuable information, if what you are feeling doesn't match up to what a chart says, it doesn't mean you are not doing it right, or that the message is not clear. I distinctly remember doing a meditation with my hands over my liver one day. I knew from Chinese medicine that the liver/gallbladder line represents anger and frustration. However, in this particular meditation I wanted to ask my liver what message it had for me without associating it through any chart. My liver gently spoke to me and gave me the message that I was not trusting in its health. The hypochondriac side of me still has issues from time to time when it comes to trusting my body's ability to simply be healthy. My liver asked me to love it, accept it, and empower it by believing that it is healthy. None of that was on any chart. That was a dialogue between my own organ and my own hand/heart/mind.

It is my goal to help you learn to listen to the messages of your own body. Our bodies always communicate with us. They are not trying to play games with us. They are trying to let us know that something is off, somewhere in some various aspect within ourselves. Our job is to stop, listen, and dive in so that we can help our body to free and release itself from within. Where our bodies choose to store pockets of exaggerated feelings or energy is something entirely individual to you.

The Carrots

When I work with a person's body, traumas present themselves to my hands and to my mental imagery as if there are rows of carrots planted deep within the system. All I see or feel is the top of the green, bushy handle sticking up. I never know just how thick the actual carrot that is embedded in the body is until I help a person pull the whole thing out. When we remove a single carrot from the muscle or fascia lines, the place that held the deep root of that carrot remains wide open and needs to be tended to and filled completely with something pure, loving, and healing. This process must be done quickly; otherwise, that open space will wreak havoc on the person's emotional and neuromuscular systems. Something happens when we remove the most significant traumas from our bodies and from what were their current narratives. We can feel incredibly naked and exposed without them. They are raw and can be painful, blistering, and volatile in their exposure depending on what the particular carrot was linked to. Each impact has become a major part of who we are. To remove any of that from our whole being is a major undertaking and should not be addressed lightly. Approach each layer slowly, thoughtfully, and mindfully.

In the world of psychology, what I see inside the body as a carrot is referred to as a *trauma capsule* in the mind. Psychologists say capsules are created at the time of life-threatening events when the mind is scared that it is going to be harmed or die, and that everything happening at the moment is locked into the subconscious mind inside a trauma capsule. Trauma capsules contain everything connected to the life-threatening event, including sights, sounds, feelings, touch, and smells that are experienced at the time of the event or attack.[9] To me, a trauma capsule is something kept inside the mind, and the carrot is what is dropped into the body at the time of the event. Remember that the mind does not work without the body, and the body does not work without the mind. However, they do not necessarily work in the same manner.

From PTSD to PTG

It is possible that one can go from post-traumatic stress disorder (PTSD) to post-traumatic growth (PTG). That is our goal with this work. PTG is the experience of individuals whose development, at least in some areas, has surpassed what was present before the struggle with crises occurred.[10] It is entirely possible to come out even stronger and better than we were before certain traumas occurred. We are not trying to go back to who we were before any incident; we are trying to bridge the gap between who that person was with the clarity and strength that we have moving forward in creating a realistic and stronger version of ourselves.

Let Us Begin

We will begin with the meditation practice for trauma, which is followed by the journal prompt to help you remember what occurred and affirm your next moves on your journey. Because we focus on only one carrot per practice, you are encouraged to repeat each meditation until you truly feel you have done all the work you can around each emotion before moving on to the next one. Continue to repeat each meditation practice until you clear out every carrot in your garden that is holding the same body emotion. You might have twenty trauma carrots and only two grief carrots. If this is the case, repeat the trauma meditation and fill out the journal on trauma twenty times before you move on to the shame section. There is an extra page in the back of the book. You can also print out more sheets or get a second notebook if you need to. This is your practice to put into action. There is a blank body image at the top of the journal so you can draw an X over the area of the body where each carrot was buried.

Meditation Tips

Be sure to use the bathroom before beginning this practice. Each practice will take approximately 15 to 20 minutes to complete. Lie down in a place where you will be comfortable and not distracted. Turn down the lights, preferably having only natural light in the room. Lie down either on the floor, a couch, or a bed. If you prefer to be seated, this works as well. Be sure you are wearing nonrestrictive clothing.

Relax every part of the external body. Then relax deeper into the organs through auto-suggestion, and begin the process of doing the body scan and working with each individual carrot that presents itself for removal, replacing it with something far more loving. Keep in mind that we only work with one carrot per meditation practice. I encourage you to return to the same meditation over and over until you feel that you have cleared every carrot in your body that was planted from this one body emotion before moving on to the next set of somatic emotions. You can fill out the journal and mark on the body as you repeat each practice.

Once you remove the carrot, choose a bucket of hot liquid and also choose the color you wish to use as you fill the space with healthy material. Do not put much thought into what color you will pick for what area. Allow that to come to you naturally. Once you are finished with the meditation, you will document where you found this particular carrot in your body and the name that you gave that carrot, as well as your color choice. From there, you can look up what color resonates with that area of the body or what that color represents in terms of healing. Remember to go to www.emilyafrancisbooks.com and click on the audio link to receive the meditation.

Audio and Written Meditation

Allow your legs to relax and your feet to fall naturally to each side. Bring your arms out slightly from the body and have the palms facing up. Allow your arms and your legs to be far enough from the center line of your body that they can comfortably lie straight without tension. Allow your arms and legs to hang like the limbs of a rag doll. Notice that they are beginning to feel heavy and limp. Feel your spine lengthen and roll itself out long against the surface beneath you. Gently turn your head from side to side, trying to touch each ear to the surface beneath you, and then settle comfortably in the middle. Exhale all the breath from your body first. Then gently take a slow, comfortable, full breath in through the nose, and exhale completely through the mouth. Make the sound *ahhh* on the first deep exhalation to signal to the nervous system that it is time to relax and let go. Breathe in, 1 . . . 2 . . . 3 . . . 4 . . . Hold the breath without tension in your body. Exhale, 1 . . . 2 . . . 3 . . . 4 . . . 5 . . . 6 . . . 7 . . . 8 . . . Hold that space, having your breath fully released before inhaling again. Inhale, 1 . . . 2 . . . 3 . . . 4 . . . Hold the breath in without tension. Slowly and gently exhale, 1 . . . 2 . . . 3 . . . 4 . . . 5 . . . 6 . . . 7 . . . 8 . . ., and again hold that space before inhaling. Keep this pace as you allow your breath to set the tone for your relaxation. Do not let your breath make you feel anxious, but instead use your breath to guide your body into letting go.

Begin with your feet and tighten them by pointing and flexing them up and down slowly to the rhythm of your breath. Then relax your feet. Relax your shins and calf muscles. Allow your knees to soften. Feel the tops of your thighs and the back sides of your legs relax. Inhale and hold your breath. Tighten every part of the legs and feet and lift your feet one inch off the surface beneath you.

Exhale and allow your legs and feet to drop. Slowly inhale and clench your buttocks, then lift your buttocks and hips off the surface beneath you. Hold your breath as you lift up and tighten the muscles. Exhale, and slowly lower down and tuck your hips under you, allowing your lower back to lie flat on the surface beneath you. Inhale and hold your breath, arch your back, and lift your entire middle and upper back off the surface beneath you. Exhale and slowly lower down. Inhale and lift your shoulders up toward your ears. Hold your breath as your shoulders are raised toward your ears. Exhale and lower your shoulders down. Inhale and hold the breath. Tighten your arms and make a fist with your hands. Lift your arms and hands one inch off the surface beneath you. Exhale and feel the heat and heaviness unwind from the tops of your shoulders, down your upper arms, around the elbows, the forearms and wrists, into the palms of your hands, and off each fingertip as you lower your arms down and relax your hands and each finger. Wiggle your fingers and then relax the entire hand. Inhale and hold your breath. Squeeze your face, tighten your eyelids, and clench your jaw. Exhale and relax your face. Inhale and hold your breath for a moment. Exhale, open your mouth, stick your tongue out as far as you can while making the *ahhh* sound as you open your eyes wide, and try to bring the eyebrows up to the top of the hairline. Relax your face and close your eyes comfortably. Relax your jaw and your lips. Rest your tongue gently, either at the roof of your mouth or the bottom of your mouth. Feel your ears soften, your cheeks relax, your chin relax. Relax your eyebrows and forehead. Relax your nose and your nostrils. Relax your scalp and every hair on your head. Breathe slowly and deeply without pressure. Gently bring your awareness all the way up and down your entire physical body, making sure that every part of your body is completely and utterly relaxed.

Allow your mind only to wander deeper into your body now. Going through the organs of the body, we will use an autosuggestion to relax your organs. Repeat in your mind after me:

Relax my physical body. My body is relaxing. My body is relaxed.
Relax my bladder. My bladder is relaxing. My bladder is relaxed.

Relax my reproductive organs. My reproductive organs are relaxing. My reproductive organs are relaxed.

Relax my small and large intestines. My intestines are relaxing. My intestines are relaxed.

Relax my stomach and pancreas. My stomach and pancreas are relaxing. My stomach and pancreas are relaxed.

Relax my spleen. My spleen is relaxing. My spleen is relaxed.

Relax my liver and gallbladder. My liver and gallbladder are relaxing. My liver and gallbladder are relaxed.

Relax my kidneys and adrenal glands. My kidneys and adrenal glands are relaxing. My kidneys and adrenal glands are relaxed.

Relax my lungs. My lungs are relaxing. My lungs are relaxed.

Relax my heart. My heart is relaxing. My heart is relaxed.

Relax my brain. My brain is relaxing. My brain is relaxed.

Relax all the organs in my body. All my organs are relaxing. All my organs are relaxed.

Relax my mind. I am slowing down my thoughts. I am calming down my feelings. My mind is deeply and completely relaxed.

Relax my entire body. My entire body is relaxing. My entire body is relaxed.

Now bring your awareness into the deepest, darkest, most hidden parts of your body. Go into the bloodstream now and gently surf through your body, through the blood and plasma. Use this liquid flow to guide you throughout your entire body one full time. Become an observer of the way in which your body flows beneath the surface. Bring yourself into the darkness where the master factory of the muscles, fasciae, and other soft tissues are working to keep you alive and healthy. Once you have scanned and surfed through your own flow of movement within, allow your vision to turn inside and go anywhere that your body asks you to go. We begin to scan the entire body all the way from the top of the head to the bottoms of the feet. Go deeper into the layer that is almost never seen, into your sacred garden. All we can see is deep, dark soil laid out through every channel of the body. This is the deepest layer of our being, where only the garden lives. Look for the rows of carrots. Look closely as you begin to notice the greenery of very small carrot tops just above the surface. Discover your garden however you like, whether by walking slowly up and down the lines of the soil, scanning only through your eyes, or gently moving your hands across the body soil in search of green bunches from the tops of the carrots. It is your practice and your choice on how to connect deeply into the spaces where you have planted your harvest. We set our intentions in this deep space that our body opens up to us and unites with our consciousness.

Think of the word ***trauma***. We now open ourselves up to any messages, images, or flashes of light or color that catch our eyes and direct them to what comes with the thought of *trauma*. Notice that when that word enters your consciousness, one flash will light up from somewhere deep inside your garden. Look for the green leafy top of the carrot that has alerted you to its presence. Bring all your awareness to this one carrot. Imagine a tiny version of yourself coming next to this carrot and sitting down beside it. None of this should be approached quickly. Each carrot has planted itself into the area and grown deep roots from the time of its inception. Be gentle as you look, listen, and ask this carrot to tell you how it got there. Allow the carrot representing this particular *trauma* to tell you its story. Allow this little carrot with deep roots to share its story with you. Your job in this moment is to do nothing but be willing to listen to it and connect with it. No judgment. No opinions. Just be open to hear what it has to tell you.

Once it shares with you an image or an actual story, feel free to give that carrot a name. Name it something to ensure that its story is heard and that you understand its meaning. Ask the carrot, by its new name, if it would be all right if you pulled it out from the roots and filled the empty area with something soothing, healing, and more loving. Explain to the carrot that it is no longer helpful for it to live there and that you can have great healing if you can move it someplace outside this body. Let that carrot know that this is to help your body come alive into radiant health. Remind the carrot that its story has value and you honor this moment and appreciate that it was so willing to share itself and be vulnerable with you. Once you feel it is safe and that the carrot has given you permission to pull it out from the deep roots, see yourself taking one hand and placing your palm tightly around the bunch, as close to the carrot itself as you can get. Gently, but with strong intention, pull the entire carrot out of its place from deep within your garden. Be sure all the roots come out with it. Take a moment to really evaluate the size, shape, and feeling of the hole that remains in its place. Take a few deep breaths, and then, with your other hand, choose a bucket of hot liquid to fill this raw, open space quickly and fully. Choose from red, orange, yellow, green, blue, purple, or white. Whatever color you choose is entirely your choice. Pour the bucket's contents into the open space. Watch how quickly the liquid hardens into an opaque crystallized material that radiates its color and its light throughout your entire body. Notice that immediately the cells from just below where the roots were have begun to light up with the opaque color and move with a whole new vibration. Place a single word of intention into this area to grow and radiate out into your body. Affirm that this intention will now grow and heal inside you. Trust the offering that you just gave to yourself. In this moment of time and space, accept your full permission to heal.

Breathe deeply into this space, and when you are ready, take your awareness, still holding the carrot that you removed in your hand, and bring your thoughts up a few layers with the breath until you can feel the air on your skin. In your mind, take the carrot that you removed from the garden and discard it as you see fit. Don't eat it. Plant it in a new garden outside yourself, or leave it outside not planted as an offering to the animals. Create a scenario where that carrot that was so full of pain and *trauma* is now recycled and used for something more positive someplace outside you. Breathe slowly and deeply and keep your eyes closed until the very end. Externalize your awareness and feel the air becoming cooler with each breath. Feel the air around your nostrils and on your skin. Bring yourself back into the room. Gently wiggle your fingers and toes. Lift your arms up and overhead and push your heels away. Stretch and lengthen your entire body. When you are ready, open your eyes and return, return, return.

Journal

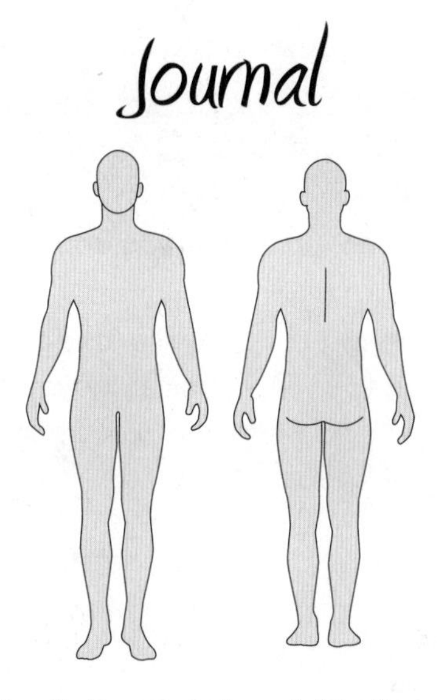

Mark an X where your body was holding the carrot.

Trauma Q&A

5-4-3-2-1 Sensory Practice for the Specific Trauma

Since we can't assume how our brains encode our various experiences, we want to go deep into the scene that our body just showed us. This will help bring it into clear vision in order to disconnect the language loop that our brains and minds have been telling us. Fill in these sensory answers before going directly into the scene that your body just shared with you in order to bring it all into the present. We will do a 5-4-3-2-1 practice to gain information from each sensory perception of the experience.

Visual aspect: Name five things that you can see in the scene your body showed you.

Look around the space. What can you see? Be very specific.

1 ______________________________

2 ______________________________

3 ______________________________

4 ______________________________

5 ______________________________

Tactile aspect: Name four things you could *touch* in that space.

This includes yourself; what you are sitting, standing, or lying on; maybe the clothes you were wearing; or someone else if they were present. You could list them as well as anything nearby in your memory of the space.

1 ______________________________

2 ______________________________

3 ______________________________

4 ______________________________

Auditory aspect: Name three things you can *hear* in that space.

This could be your voice, someone else's voice, music in the background, or sounds outside your space. Tune in deeply to what sounds are around you in the space your body showed you.

1 ______________________________

2 ______________________________

3 ______________________________

Olfactory aspect: Name two things you can *smell* in that space.

If you were outside or inside, what was around you that you can identify with a scent?

1 ______________________________

2 ______________________________

Gustatory aspect: Name one thing you could *taste* in your mouth during that time.

This could be a food you ate just before the session, a drink, or chewing gum. It could be another person or thing if they invaded your space or mouth. As an example, in a car accident, I distinctly remember the taste of metal in my mouth as if I had eaten aluminum foil. When you sit with this idea of which tastes you were able to identify, the scene becomes more present.

____

What was the story that the carrot shared with you?

____

What carrot presented itself to you when you meditated on the concept of trauma?

____

Where was that carrot located in the body?

____

How did it show itself to you?

____

How was it different (if it was different) from the story that you identify with in that particular circumstance?

____

Did you learn anything from what the carrot had to share with you?

____

Circle the color you chose to replace the carrot with and discuss why that color came to your mind.

You can reference the chart on page 98 to see what each color signifies.

RED ORANGE YELLOW GREEN BLUE PURPLE WHITE

What name did you give to the carrot for this story?

___

How do you feel in your body after removing the carrot from its rooted place?

___

Affirmation: *Create a simple affirmation to help enforce that it is safe for you to heal.*

___

___

Example affirmations: *It is safe for me to explore the messages of my body.*

I trust the messages of my body.

It is within my own power to heal from this trauma now.

Pairing the Affirmation with a Hand Position or Mudra

When we create an affirmation to repeat following our deep meditation work, it is important that we also pair the practice with a specific touch to our body to fully activate and align both the tissue memory patterns and the mental groove sets. There are many options to help us dialogue deeply with the body. Feel free to explore all these suggestions and choose the one that works best for you and your specific work.

The two-hand touch involves placing the left middle fingertip directly over your navel. The left hand is the receiving hand. In Chinese medicine this is the CV8 point. The CV8 translates to the "spirit gate." This is a point of integration to help recalibrate your current energy to match the vibrational remedy that is placed upon it.[12] Place the tip of your right middle finger at the very top of your head at the midline. The right hand is considered the giving hand. This point in Chinese medicine is known as the *baijiu* or the DU20 point. This point translates to "the meeting of the hundreds." It is the place where all the energies within the body converge and meet.[13]

An affirmation while holding the hands in these two positions is "I am healthy and I am safe." A more detailed affirmation might be needed according to the work that you have just completed. The affirmation you choose is entirely up to you.

Prayer hands is the most notable hand position or mudra known worldwide to prepare and activate our connection to the heavens as well as to activate the clearing of the mind and the opening of the heart space. Prayer hands asks that God enter our work and help us to clear and heal.

Mudras include touching together specific fingers to activate a certain energy and intention. The most basic hand mudra besides prayer hands is to connect the first finger to the thumb (chin mudra) to connect yourself with the universe. It is a gesture of consciousness. The index finger represents you, and the thumb represents the universe. How you naturally place the two fingers together can give insight into where you are in relation with the universe. If you tuck the finger under the thumb, this indicates that you are bowing down to the universe. Meeting tip to tip would indicate that you feel even with the universe, not above or beneath the energy itself.

This is ultimately your practice. When creating an affirmation, choose any of these to confirm the dialogue within the body.

Chapter 2

Shame

Oh shame . . . how well so many of us know you. Shame can be such an intimate partner when we don't know how to shake it. Shame is a pattern that so many of us have laced ourselves up with as a constant behavior pattern, which so many of us have resorted to and placed upon ourselves time and again.

The word *shame* means to feel mortified, painfully embarrassed, self-loathing, or like you are a bad person. When I try to describe how the emotion of shame feels to my hands when I feel it in someone else, it's hard to explain. It's as if the tissues themselves take on a different constitution. Shame makes the body cry. That is the best way that I can explain it. Shame is something that was not created inside you, but something that was put into you, and then you assumed the responsibility of taking it over and repeating the shame talk as you hammered it down into the tissues and cells within.

The Upside to Shame?

There is absolutely no upside to shame unless you consider the growth in rejecting behaviors associated with shame. When you learn that the hot coal that someone throws at you does not have anything to do with you, it allows you to choose whether or not to catch it, plant it, or drop it. But this comes later. Shame is incredibly toxic to the body and mind. Shame makes our muscles and body tissues weep. It becomes difficult to stand upright without hunching our shoulders and looking down more often than looking up or straight into anyone's eyes, most notably our own. The mirror can be a hefty source of shame and loathing when we are not balanced and free from our internal dialogue at its worst. Our minds perceive shame in a very heavy, sorrowful context, like we are being punished. Internally, shame is experienced much deeper. Shame cuts deep and stores itself heavily in the body. Have you ever noticed the trees on the days it's going to rain and the leaves begin to turn down? That's what I imagine in our bodies—in the cells, the tissues, the muscles—when we bring shame into ourselves. Everything turns down in sorrow and begins to gently weep. Shame to me is something that comes from outside ourselves and then anchors down based on the way someone else speaks to us or treats us. As a general rule in body work, shame is really hard to work with and release because of the deeply held disdain for wanting to discuss the reasons behind our experiences of shame. No one ever likes to say out loud the way that someone has made them feel or what was actually said or done.

Unfortunately, when someone else throws something ugly at us, we choose to take it on and continue it in a talk cycle that never changes back to its original track. Someone could say one hurtful thing to us or about us along with twenty positive things, and the only one we take into our bodies and hold down would be that one line that created the experience of shame. Understand that we always have the choice either to take the feelings of shame in and anchor down with it or to let it roll off and not take anything personally from toxic people. This is a sign of maturity and awareness that things that come at us from someplace else are not ours to own. This comes with work. It is never gained freely.

I had an eighth-grade math teacher who found out I went to a tutor to help me pass the course and announced to the whole class that I was "a stupid little cheerleader who can't pass math and had to get a tutor." It was mortifying. The words in that statement have never wavered in my retelling of that story. It's not a summary of what he said. They were his exact words. They are etched into a groove in my mind forever. From the moment of impact, it became my constant internal talking reel. I believed his words for a great many years to come. I felt tiny, ashamed, and embarrassed, and they became the words that defined me. He defined me, and I allowed it. I have let so many people define me over the years. I've given my power away time and again. Shame can lead to self-harm or self-punishment very easily. People punish their feelings of shame through food restriction or indulgence, alcohol or drug use, cutting, or other self-harming actions or self-mutilation. The reaction to shame is not to do something to anyone outside ourselves. It becomes a repeating internal beatdown. Shame becomes something we take upon ourselves, and we become the executioners of our own bodies and mental patterns. Shame is powerful and private and so poisonous to our bodies and our souls.

Wanting to Heal Versus Doing the Healing

Even if we truly want to heal, wanting it and doing the work required to achieve it are very far apart in effort. The many healers who I went to in order to recover from my extreme anxiety and panic always left me with this amazing feeling of hope that I had been healed. I found, however, that few practices did the work of refilling that space from which they had removed the original experience. In just days, I found myself almost trying to pull it back to me. I hated those fear behaviors, but I also had no idea how to live without them. It became a cycle of addiction until I learned to fill those spaces with something equally as fulfilling, equally as weighty in its feeling within my body, and stronger than choosing the pain over the power. As a disclaimer, which I also mention in the overview, please understand that I am in no way trying to minimize the work that must be done to heal well. This book is meant to address the physical and emotional aspects of the body and the way that the body stores its pains, shames, guilts, griefs, and traumas. If there is a significant disconnect within the mind and brain (the brain is an organ, and the mind is the place where your thoughts and behaviors live), please see a professional psychologist (for therapy to help with the mind) or a psychiatrist (for medical therapy to help regulate the brain receptors) to help you access the proper environment in which your whole body will be able to fully heal. Treating the mind, the brain, and the body will give you your best chance of recovering fully and reclaiming your life in the biggest and brightest ways possible. In my greatest time of need, medication saved me. I do not advocate taking medication, but I most certainly am not against it, either. The route you need for your healing is extremely individual. I offer this information because I do not want anyone to feel ashamed should they need to seek outside help, therapy, or medication. This book comes as an offering to help you work from the space within your body. My intention is to help you live peacefully within your body for the rest of your life.

Meditation Tips

Be sure to use the bathroom before beginning this practice. Each practice will take approximately 15 to 20 minutes to complete. Lie down in a place where you will be comfortable and not distracted. Turn down the lights, preferably having only natural light in the room. Lie down either on the floor, a couch, or a bed. If you prefer to be seated, this works as well. Be sure you are wearing nonrestrictive clothing.

Relax every part of the external body. Then relax deeper into the organs through auto-suggestion, and begin the process of doing the body scan and working with each individual carrot that presents itself for removal, replacing it with something far more loving. Keep in mind that we only work with one carrot per meditation practice. I encourage you to return to the same meditation over and over until you feel that you have cleared every carrot in your body that was planted from this one body emotion before moving on to the next set of somatic emotions. You can fill out the journal and mark on the body as you repeat each practice.

Once you remove the carrot, choose a bucket of hot liquid and also choose the color you wish to use as you fill the space with healthy material. Do not put much thought into what color you will pick for what area. Allow that to come to you naturally. Once you are finished with the meditation you will document where you found this particular carrot in your body and the name that you gave that carrot as well as your color choice. From there, you can look up what color resonates with that area of the body or what that color represents in terms of healing. Remember to go to www.emilyafrancisbooks.com and click on the audio link to receive the meditation.

Audio and Written Meditation

Allow your legs to relax and your feet to fall naturally to each side. Bring your arms out slightly from the body and have the palms facing up. Allow your arms and your legs to be far enough from the center line of your body that they can comfortably lie straight without tension. Allow your arms and legs to hang like the limbs of a rag doll. Notice that they are beginning to feel heavy and limp. Feel your spine lengthen and roll itself out long against the surface beneath you. Gently turn your head from side to side, trying to touch each ear to the surface beneath you, and then settle comfortably in the middle. Exhale all the breath from your body first. Then, gently take a slow, comfortable, full breath in through the nose and exhale completely through the mouth. Make the sound *ahhh* on the first deep exhalation to signal to the nervous system that it is time to relax and let go. Breathe in, 1 . . . 2 . . . 3 . . . 4 . . . Hold the breath without tension in your body. Exhale, 1 . . . 2 . . . 3 . . . 4 . . . 5 . . . 6 . . . 7 . . . 8 . . . Hold that space, having your breath fully released before inhaling again. Inhale, 1 . . . 2 . . . 3 . . . 4 . . . Hold the breath in without tension. Slowly and gently exhale 1 . . . 2 . . . 3 . . . 4 . . . 5 . . . 6 . . . 7 . . . 8 . . . and again hold that space before inhaling. Keep this pace as you allow your breath to set the tone for your relaxation. Do not let your breath make you feel anxious, but instead use your breath to guide your body into letting go.

Begin with your feet and tighten them by pointing and flexing them up and down slowly to the rhythm of your breath. Then, relax your feet. Relax your shins and calf muscles. Allow your knees to soften. Feel the tops of your thighs and the back sides of your legs relax. Inhale and hold your breath. Tighten every part of the legs and feet and lift your feet one inch off the surface beneath you. Exhale and allow your legs and feet to drop. Slowly inhale and clench your buttocks, then lift your buttocks and hips off the surface beneath you. Hold your breath as you lift up and tighten the muscles. Exhale, and slowly lower down and tuck your hips under you, allowing your lower back to lie flat on the surface beneath you. Inhale and hold your breath, arch your back, and lift your entire middle and upper back off the surface beneath you. Exhale and slowly lower down. Inhale and lift your shoulders up toward your ears. Hold your breath as your shoulders are raised up toward your ears. Exhale and lower your shoulders down. Inhale and hold the breath. Tighten your arms and make a fist with your hands. Lift your arms and hands one inch off the surface beneath you. Exhale and feel the heat and heaviness unwind from the tops of your shoulders, down your upper arms, around the elbows, the forearms and wrists, into the palms of your hands, and off each fingertip as you lower your arms down and relax your hands and each finger. Wiggle your fingers and then relax the entire hand. Inhale and hold your breath. Squeeze your face, tighten your eyelids, and clench your jaw. Exhale and relax your face. Inhale and hold your breath for a moment. Exhale, open your mouth, stick your tongue out as far as you can while making the *ahhh* sound as you open your eyes wide, and try to bring the eyebrows up to the top of the hairline. Relax your face and close your eyes comfortably. Relax your jaw and your lips. Rest your tongue gently, either at the roof of your mouth or the bottom of your mouth. Feel your ears soften, your cheeks relax, your chin relax. Relax your eyebrows and forehead. Relax your nose and your nostrils. Relax your scalp and every hair on your head. Breathe slowly and deeply without pressure. Gently bring your awareness all the way up and down your entire physical body, making sure that every part of your body is completely and utterly relaxed.

Allow your mind only to wander deeper into your body now. Going through the organs of the body, we will use an auto-suggestion to relax our organs. Repeat in your mind after me:

Relax my physical body. My body is relaxing. My body is relaxed.

Relax my bladder. My bladder is relaxing. My bladder is relaxed.

Relax my reproductive organs. My reproductive organs are relaxing. My reproductive organs are relaxed.

Relax my small and large intestines. My intestines are relaxing. My intestines are relaxed.

Relax my stomach and pancreas. My stomach and pancreas are relaxing. My stomach and pancreas are relaxed.

Relax my spleen. My spleen is relaxing. My spleen is relaxed.

Relax my liver and gallbladder. My liver and gallbladder are relaxing. My liver and gallbladder are relaxed.

Relax my kidneys and adrenal glands. My kidneys and my adrenal glands are relaxing. My kidneys and adrenal glands are relaxed.

Relax my lungs. My lungs are relaxing. My lungs are relaxed.

Relax my heart. My heart is relaxing. My heart is relaxed.

Relax my brain. My brain is relaxing. My brain is relaxed.

Relax all the organs in my body. All my organs are relaxing. All my organs are relaxed.

Relax my mind. I am slowing down my thoughts. I am calming down my feelings. My mind is deeply and completely relaxed.

Relax my entire body. My entire body is relaxing. My entire body is relaxed.

Now bring your awareness into the deepest, darkest, most hidden parts of your body. Go into the bloodstream now and gently surf through your body, through the blood and plasma. Use this liquid flow to guide you throughout your entire body one full time. Become an observer of the way in which your body flows beneath the surface. Bring yourself into the darkness where the master factory of the muscles, fasciae, and other soft tissues are working to keep you alive and healthy. Once you have scanned and surfed through your own flow of movement within, allow your vision to turn inside and go anywhere that your body asks you to go. We begin to scan the entire body all the way from the top of the head to the bottoms of the feet. Go deeper into the layer that is almost never seen, into your sacred garden. All we can see is deep, dark soil laid out through every channel of your body. This is the deepest layer of our being, where only the garden lives. Look for the rows of carrots. Look closely as you begin to notice the greenery of very small carrot tops just above the surface. Discover your garden however you like, whether by walking slowly up and down the lines of the soil, scanning only through your eyes, or gently moving your hands across the body soil in search of green bunches from the tops of the carrots. It is your practice and your choice on how to connect deeply into the spaces where you have planted your harvest. We set our intentions in this deep space that our body opens up to us and unites with our consciousness.

Think of the word ***shame***. We now open ourselves up to any messages, images, or flashes of light or color that catch our eyes and direct them to what comes with the thought of *shame*. Notice that when that word enters your consciousness, one flash will light up from somewhere deep inside your garden. Look for the green leafy top of the carrot that has alerted you to its presence. Bring all your awareness to this one carrot. Imagine a tiny version of yourself coming next to this carrot and sitting down beside it. None of this should be approached quickly. Each carrot has planted itself into the area and grown deep roots from the time of its inception. Be gentle as you look, listen, and ask this carrot to tell you how it got there. Allow the carrot that represents this particular *shame* to tell you its story. Allow this little carrot with deep roots to share its story with you. Your job in this moment is to do nothing but be willing to listen to it and connect with it. No judgment. No opinions. Just be open to hear what it has to tell you.

Once it shares with you an image or an actual story, feel free to give that carrot a name. Name it something to ensure that its story is heard and that you understand its meaning. Ask the carrot, by its new name, if it would be all right if you pulled it out from the roots and filled the empty area with something soothing, healing, and more loving. Explain to the carrot that it is no longer helpful for it to live there, and that we can have great healing if we can move it someplace outside this body. Let that carrot know that this is to help your body come alive into radiant health. Remind the carrot that its story has value and you honor this moment and appreciate that it was so willing to share itself and be vulnerable with you. Once you feel it is safe and that the carrot has given you permission to pull it out from the deep roots, see yourself taking one hand and placing your palm tightly around the bunch as close to the carrot itself as you can get. Gently, but with strong intention, pull the entire carrot out of its place from deep within your garden. Be sure all the roots come out with it. Take a moment to really evaluate the size, shape, and feeling of the hole that remains in its place. Take a few deep breaths and then, with your other hand, choose a bucket of hot liquid to fill this raw, open space quickly and fully. Choose from red, orange, yellow, green, blue, purple, or white. Whatever color you choose is entirely your choice. Pour the bucket's contents into the open space. Watch how quickly the liquid hardens into an opaque crystallized material that radiates its color and its light throughout your entire body. Notice that immediately, the cells from just below where the roots were have begun to light up with the opaque color and move with a whole new vibration. Place a single word of intention into this area to grow and radiate out into your body. Affirm that this intention will now grow and heal inside you. Trust the offering that you just gave to yourself. In this moment of time and space, accept your full permission to heal.

Breathe deeply into this space, and when you are ready, take your awareness, still holding the carrot that you removed in your hand, and bring your thoughts up a few layers with the breath until you can feel the air on your skin. In your mind, take the carrot that you removed from the garden and discard it as you see fit. Don't eat it. Plant it in a new garden outside yourself or leave it outside not planted as an offering to the animals. Create a scenario where that carrot that was so full of *shame* is now recycled and used for something more positive someplace outside you. Breathe slowly and deeply and keep your eyes closed until the very end. Externalize your awareness and feel the air becoming cooler with each breath. Feel the air around your nostrils and on your skin. Bring yourself back into the room. Gently wiggle your fingers and toes. Lift your arms up and overhead and push your heels away. Stretch and lengthen your entire body. When you are ready, open your eyes and return, return, return.

Journal

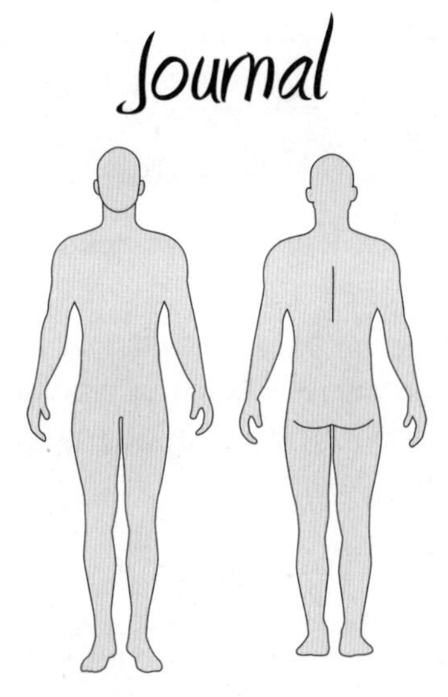

Mark an X where your body was holding the carrot.

Shame Q&A

5-4-3-2-1 Sensory Practice for Shame

Since you can't assume anything about how your brain encodes your various experiences, you want to go deep into the scene that your body just showed you. This will help bring it into clear vision in order to disconnect the language loop that your brain and mind have been telling you. Fill in these sensory answers before going directly into the scene that your body just shared with you in order to bring it all into the present. We will do a 5-4-3-2-1 practice to gain information from each sensory perception of the experience.

Visual aspect: Name five things that you can *see* in the scene your body showed you.

Look around the space. What can you see? Be very specific.

1 ____

2 ____

3 ______________________________

4 ______________________________

5 ______________________________

Tactile aspect: Name four things you could *touch* in that space.

This includes yourself, what you are sitting, standing, or lying on, maybe the clothes you were wearing, or someone else if they were present. You could list them as well as anything nearby in your memory of the space.

1 ______________________________

2 ______________________________

3 ______________________________

4 ______________________________

Auditory aspect: Name three things you can *hear* in that space.

This could be your voice, someone else's voice, music in the background, or sounds outside your space. Tune in deeply to what sounds are around you in the space your body showed you.

1 ______________________________

2 ______________________________

3 ______________________________

Olfactory aspect: Name two things you can *smell* in that space.

If you were outside or inside, what was around you that you can identify with a scent?

1 ______________________________

2 ______________________________

Gustatory aspect: Name one thing you could *taste* in your mouth during that time.

This could be a food you ate just before the session, a drink, or chewing gum. It could be another person or thing if they invaded your space or mouth. As an example, in a car accident. I distinctly remember the taste of metal in my mouth as if I had eaten aluminum foil. When you sit with this idea of which tastes you were able to identify, the scene becomes more present.

____

What was the story that the carrot shared with you?

____

What carrot presented itself to you when you meditated on the concept of shame?

____

Where was that carrot located in the body?

____

How did it show itself to you?

____

How was it different (if it was different) from the story that you identify with in that particular circumstance?

____

Did you learn anything from what the carrot had to share with you?

____

Circle the color you chose to replace the carrot with and discuss why that color came to your mind.

You can reference the chart at the end of Section I to see what each color signifies.

RED ORANGE YELLOW GREEN BLUE PURPLE WHITE

What name did you give to the carrot for this story?

____

How do you feel in your body after removing the carrot from its rooted place?

____

Affirmation: *Create a simple affirmation to help enforce that it is safe for you to heal.*

____

____

Example affirmations: *It is safe for me to explore the messages of my body.*

I trust the messages of my body.

It is within my own power to heal and release feelings of shame now.

Pairing the Affirmation with a Hand Position or Mudra

When we create an affirmation to repeat following our deep meditation work, it is important that we also pair the practice with a specific touch to our body to fully activate and align both the tissue memory patterns and the mental groove sets. There are many options to help us dialogue deeply with the body. Feel free to explore all these suggestions and choose the one that works best for you and your specific work. My top suggestions are:

The two-hand touch involves placing the left middle fingertip directly over your navel. The left hand is the receiving hand. In Chinese medicine this is the CV8 point. The CV8 translates to the "spirit gate." This is a point of integration to help recalibrate your current energy to match the vibrational remedy that is placed upon it.[12]

Place the tip of your right middle finger at the very top of your head at the midline. The right hand is considered the giving hand. This point in Chinese medicine is known as the *baijiu* or the DU20 point. This point translates to "the meeting of the hundreds." It is the place where all the energies within the body converge and meet.[13]

An affirmation you can say while holding the hands in these two positions is: "I am healthy, and I am safe." A more detailed affirmation might be needed according to the work that you have just completed. The affirmation you choose is entirely up to you.

Prayer hands is the most notable hand position or mudra known worldwide to prepare and activate our connection to the heavens as well as to activate the clearing of the mind and the opening of the heart space. Prayer hands asks that God enter our work and help us to clear and heal.

Mudras include touching together specific fingers to activate a certain energy and intention. The most basic hand mudra besides prayer hands is to connect the first finger to the thumb (chin mudra) to connect yourself with the universe. It is a gesture of consciousness. The index finger represents you, and the thumb represents the universe. How you naturally place the two fingers together can give insight into where you are in relation with the universe. If you tuck

the finger under the thumb, this indicates that you are bowing down to the universe. Meeting tip to tip would indicate that you feel even the universe: not above or beneath the energy itself.

This is ultimately your practice. When creating an affirmation, choose any of these to confirm the dialogue within the body.

Chapter 3
Guilt

Guilt is shame's dysfunctional best friend. We have all had that friend in our lives who always causes trouble. Our mischievous friend is sometimes fun to have in our lives, but when it comes to guilt and shame, that is not the case. Think of guilt as shame's abusive boyfriend or girlfriend. If shame is into self-punishment, guilt is into the repetitive cycle of abuse. You know those gaslighters who are totally narcissistic and love to keep you down? They never want you to be happy and have a deep attachment to whether or not you are functioning well, and they always root for not? That name is guilt in this scenario. Guilt keeps you broken. It can be paralyzing to many with too much guilt running through their veins. Guilt is heavy and hardens our bodies' tissues. As I refer to shame in the body as the leaves that turn down before the rain, guilt is the booming thunder or the scary crashing lightning bolts. Guilt's self-talk is nasty business. Guilt is not an internal shaming and beatdown like shame; however, their self-talk can be quite interchangeable.

Guilt is an emotion stemming from you to something outside yourself. It might even be a nasty behavior that you do and the feelings that accompany that action after you realize you have deeply wounded someone. "It's all my fault" is a common statement we say to ourselves when we feel guilt. Things like, "Why do I always do this, I always mess things up, I'm so stupid, I'm so . . ." Guilt can present as a heavy sensation, like a bowling ball inside your body that you walk around with all the time. Guilt can be a very manipulative behavior, especially when used to gain control over someone or something. We've all done it. We've all used guilt as our secret weapon to talk someone into something we wanted them to do. It's such an easy behavior to resort to. We use guilt often to get people to comply, children especially. Parents are notorious for creating guilt in their children to get them to do what they have been told. People feel guilt according to their sense of right and wrong. It's the if/then approach to life that we are so familiar with. This can include various religious practices, health practices, or other either/or scenarios that come with pretty hefty guilt behaviors either at you or from you. *If* you don't follow the rules, *then* you are a bad person. Then you take that into yourself and think you are a bad person and now you have brought in shame.

Shame and guilt are intertwined most of the time. It's very hard to find guilt without shame. When working with guilt in terms of body healing, it can be a little bit easier to lift from ourselves than shame. Liberating ourselves from guilt is working to rid ourselves of the behavior and the talk. Liberation from shame is more trying to lift it out of the body tissues that actually dialogue within themselves, and that is very difficult to do. Guilt can harden inside us, and then we can pick up the pieces. Imagine that inside your body is a little snake. It slithers all around your insides, traveling through your blood, hiding around the muscle. Now the snake needs to lay eggs. It finds a safe place deep inside the body, perhaps on a cushion of muscle tissue that feels like a cozy warm bed. The snakes have not hatched and are still in egg form. The eggs are guilt. You can pick them up; they are still whole pieces to work with. Now imagine those eggs have already hatched and the shells are getting absorbed into the body; that is what it's like to remove the shame. There are many small pieces, not easy to pick up and remove, but the tie-in to guilt is extremely similar. They have the same origin, but not the same form.

Meditation Tips

Be sure to use the bathroom before beginning this practice. Each practice will take approximately 15 to 20 minutes to complete. Lie down in a place where you will be comfortable and not distracted. Turn down the lights, preferably having only natural light in the room. Lie down either on the floor, a couch, or a bed. If you prefer to be seated, this works as well. Be sure you are wearing nonrestrictive clothing.

Relax every part of the external body. Then relax deeper into the organs through auto-suggestion and begin the process of doing the body scan and working with each individual carrot that presents itself for removal, replacing it with something far more loving. Keep in mind that we only work with one carrot per meditation practice. I encourage you to return to the same meditation over and over until you feel that you have cleared every carrot in your body that was planted from this one body emotion before moving on to the next set of somatic emotions. You can fill out the journal and mark on the body as you repeat each practice.

Once you remove the carrot, choose a bucket of hot liquid and also choose the color you wish to use to fill the space with healthy material. Do not put much thought into what color you will pick for what area. Allow that to come to you naturally. Once you are finished with the meditation, you will document where you found this particular carrot in your body and the name that you gave that carrot as well as your color choice. From there, you can look up what color resonates with that area of the body or what that color represents in terms of healing. Remember to go to www.emilyafrancisbooks.com and click on the audio link to receive the meditation.

Audio and Written Meditation

Allow your legs to relax and your feet to fall naturally to each side. Bring your arms out slightly from the body and have the palms facing up. Allow your arms and your legs to be far enough from the center line of your body that they can comfortably lie straight without tension. Allow your arms and legs to hang like the limbs of a rag doll. Notice that they are beginning to feel heavy and limp. Feel your spine lengthen and roll itself out long against the surface beneath you. Gently turn your head from side to side, trying to touch each ear to the surface beneath you, and then settle comfortably in the middle. Exhale all of the breath from your body first. Then, gently take a slow, comfortable, full breath in through the nose and exhale completely through the mouth. Make the sound *ahhh* on the first deep exhalation to signal to the nervous system that it is time to relax and let go. Breathe in, 1 . . . 2 . . . 3 . . . 4 . . . Hold the breath without tension in your body. Exhale, 1 . . . 2 . . . 3 . . . 4 . . . 5 . . . 6 . . . 7 . . . 8 . . . Hold that space, having your breath fully released before inhaling again. Inhale, 1 . . . 2 . . . 3 . . . 4 . . . Hold the breath in without tension. Slowly and gently exhale 1 . . . 2 . . . 3 . . . 4 . . . 5 . . . 6 . . . 7 . . . 8 . . . and again hold that space before inhaling. Keep this pace as you allow your breath to set the tone for your relaxation. Do not let your breath make you feel anxious, but instead use your breath to guide your body into letting go.

Begin with your feet and tighten them by pointing and flexing them up and down slowly to the rhythm of your breath. Then, relax your feet. Relax your shins and calf muscles. Allow your knees to soften. Feel the tops of your thighs and the back sides of your legs relax. Inhale and hold your breath. Tighten every part of the legs and feet and lift your feet one inch off the surface beneath you. Exhale and allow your legs and feet to drop. Slowly inhale and clench your buttocks, then lift your buttocks and hips off the surface beneath you. Hold your breath as you lift up and tighten the muscles. Exhale, and slowly lower down and tuck your hips under you, allowing your lower back to lie flat on the surface beneath you. Inhale and hold your breath, arch your back, and lift your entire middle and upper back off the surface beneath you. Exhale and slowly lower down. Inhale and lift your shoulders up toward your ears. Hold your breath as your shoulders are raised toward your ears. Exhale and lower your shoulders down. Inhale and hold the breath. Tighten your arms and make a fist with your hands. Lift your arms and hands one inch off the surface beneath you. Exhale and feel the heat and heaviness unwind from the tops of your shoulders, down your upper arms, around the elbows, the forearms and wrists, into the palms of your hands, and off each fingertip as you lower your arms down and relax your hands and each finger. Wiggle your fingers and then relax the entire hand. Inhale and hold your breath. Squeeze your face, tighten your eyelids, and clench your jaw. Exhale and relax your face. Inhale and hold your breath for a moment. Exhale, open your mouth, stick your tongue out as far as you can while making the *ahhh* sound as you open your eyes wide and try to bring the eyebrows up to the top of the hairline. Relax your face and close your eyes comfortably. Relax your jaw and your lips. Rest your tongue gently, either at the roof of your mouth or the bottom of your mouth. Feel your ears soften, your cheeks relax, your chin relax. Relax your eyebrows and forehead. Relax your nose and your nostrils. Relax your scalp and every hair on your head. Breathe slowly and deeply without pressure. Gently bring your awareness all the way up and down your entire physical body, making sure that every part of your body is completely and utterly relaxed.

Allow your mind only to wander deeper into your body now. Going through the organs of the body, we will use an auto-suggestion to relax our organs. Repeat in your mind after me:

Relax my physical body. My body is relaxing. My body is relaxed.
Relax my bladder. My bladder is relaxing. My bladder is relaxed.

Relax my reproductive organs. My reproductive organs are relaxing. My reproductive organs are relaxed.

Relax my small and large intestines. My intestines are relaxing. My intestines are relaxed.

Relax my stomach and pancreas. My stomach and pancreas are relaxing. My stomach and pancreas are relaxed.

Relax my spleen. My spleen is relaxing. My spleen is relaxed.

Relax my liver and gallbladder. My liver and gallbladder are relaxing. My liver and gallbladder are relaxed.

Relax my kidneys and adrenal glands. My kidneys and adrenal glands are relaxing. My kidneys and adrenal glands are relaxed.

Relax my lungs. My lungs are relaxing. My lungs are relaxed.

Relax my heart. My heart is relaxing. My heart is relaxed.

Relax my brain. My brain is relaxing. My brain is relaxed.

Relax all the organs in my body. All of my organs are relaxing. All of my organs are relaxed.

Relax my mind. I am slowing down my thoughts. I am calming down my feelings. My mind is deeply and completely relaxed.

Relax my entire body. My entire body is relaxing. My entire body is relaxed.

Now bring your awareness into the deepest, darkest, most hidden parts of your body. Go into the bloodstream now and gently surf through your body, through the blood and plasma. Use this liquid flow to guide you throughout your entire body one full time. Become an observer of the way in which your body flows beneath the surface. Bring yourself into the darkness where the master factory of the muscles, fasciae, and other soft tissues are working to keep you alive and healthy. Once you have scanned and surfed through your own flow of movement within, allow your vision to turn inside and go anywhere that your body asks you to go. We begin to scan the entire body all the way from the top of the head to the bottoms of the feet. Go deeper into the layer that is almost never seen, into your sacred garden. All we can see is deep, dark soil laid out through every channel of your body. This is the deepest layer of our being, where only the garden lives. Look for the rows of carrots. Look closely as you begin to notice the greenery of very small carrot tops just above the surface. Discover your garden however you like, whether by walking slowly up and down the lines of the soil, scanning only through your eyes, or gently moving your hands across the body soil in search of green bunches from the tops of the carrots. It is your practice and your choice on how to connect deeply into the spaces where you have planted your harvest. We set our intentions in this deep space that our body opens up to us and unites with our consciousness.

Think of the word ***guilt***. We now open ourselves up to any messages, images, or flashes of light or color that catch our eyes and direct them to what comes with the thought of *guilt*. Notice that when that word enters your consciousness, one flash will light up from somewhere deep inside your garden. Look for the green leafy top of the carrot that has alerted you to its presence. Bring all your awareness to this one carrot. Imagine a tiny version of yourself coming next to this carrot and sitting down beside it. None of this should be approached quickly. Each carrot has planted itself into the area and grown deep roots from the time of its inception. Be gentle as you look, listen, and ask this carrot to tell you how it got there. Allow the carrot that represents this particular *guilt* to tell you its story. Allow this little carrot with deep roots to share its story with you. Your job in this moment is to do nothing but be willing to listen to it and connect with it. No judgment. No opinions. Just be open to hear what it has to tell you.

Once it shares with you an image or an actual story, feel free to give that carrot a name. Name it something to ensure that its story is heard and that you understand its meaning. Ask the carrot, by its new name, if it would be all right if you pulled it out from the roots and filled the empty area with something soothing, healing, and more loving. Explain to the carrot that it is no longer helpful for it to live there and that you can have great healing if you can move it to be used someplace outside this body. Let that carrot know that this is to help your body come alive into radiant health. Remind the carrot that its story has value and you honor this moment and appreciate that it was so willing to share itself and be vulnerable with you. Once you feel it is safe and that the carrot has given you permission to pull it out from the deep roots, see yourself taking one hand and placing your palm tightly around the bunch as close to the carrot itself as you can get. Gently, but with strong intention, pull the entire carrot out of its place from deep within your garden. Be sure all the roots come out with it. Take a moment to really evaluate the size, shape, and feeling of the hole that remains in its place. Take a few deep breaths and then, with your other hand, choose a bucket of hot liquid to fill this raw, open space quickly and fully. Choose from red, orange, yellow, green, blue, purple, or white. Whatever color you choose is entirely your choice. Pour the bucket's contents into the open space. Watch how quickly the liquid hardens into an opaque crystallized material that radiates its color and its light throughout your entire body. Notice that immediately, the cells from just below where the roots were have begun to light up with the opaque color and move with a whole new vibration. Place a single word of intention into this area to grow and radiate out into your body. Affirm that this intention will now grow and heal inside you. Trust the offering that you just gave to yourself. In this moment of time and space, accept your full permission to heal.

Breathe deeply into this space and when you are ready, take your awareness, still holding the carrot that you removed in your hand, and bring your thoughts up a few layers with the breath until you can feel the air on your skin. In your mind, take the carrot that you removed from the garden and discard it as you see fit. Don't eat it. Plant it in a new garden outside of yourself or leave it outside not planted as an offering to the animals. Create a scenario where that carrot that was so full of *guilt* will be recycled and used for something more positive someplace outside of you. Breathe slowly and deeply, and keep your eyes closed until the very end. Externalize your awareness and feel the air becoming cooler with each breath. Feel the air around your nostrils and on your skin. Bring yourself back into the room. Gently wiggle your fingers and toes. Lift your arms up and overhead and push your heels away. Stretch and lengthen your entire body. When you are ready, open your eyes and return, return, return.

Journal

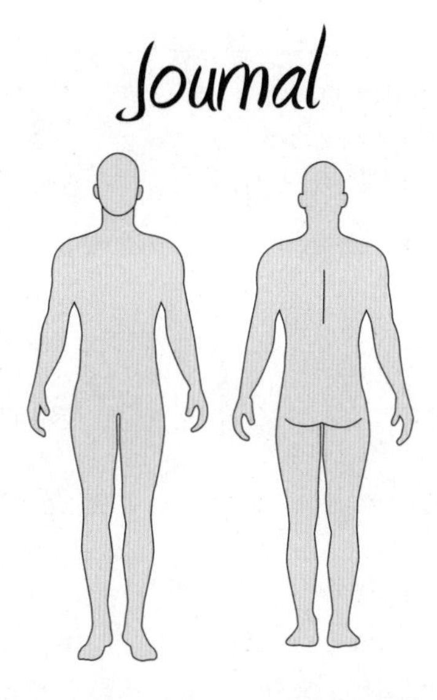

Mark an X where your body was holding the carrot.

Guilt Q&A

5-4-3-2-1 Sensory Practice for Guilt

Since we can't assume how our brains encode our various experiences, we want to go deep into the scene that our body just showed us. This will help bring it into clear vision in order to disconnect the language loop that our brain and mind have been telling us. Fill in these sensory answers before going directly into the scene that your body just shared with you in order to bring it all into the present. We will do a 5-4-3-2-1 practice to gain information from each sensory perception of the experience.

Visual aspect: Name five things that you can *see* in the scene your body showed you. Look around the space. What can you see? Be very specific.

1 ______________________________

2 ______________________________

3 ______________________________

4 ______________________________

5 ______________________________

Tactile aspect: Name four things you could *touch* in that space.

This includes yourself, what you are sitting, standing, or lying on, maybe the clothes you were wearing, or someone else if they were present. You could list them as well as anything nearby in your memory of the space.

1 ______________________________

2 ______________________________

3 ______________________________

4 ______________________________

Auditory aspect: Name three things you can *hear* in that space.

This could be your voice, someone else's voice, music in the background, or sounds outside of your space. Tune in deeply to what sounds are around you in the space your body showed you.

1 ______________________________

2 ______________________________

3 ______________________________

Olfactory aspect: Name two things you can *smell* in that space.

If you were outside or inside, what was around you that you can identify with a scent?

1 ______________________________

2 ______________________________

Gustatory aspect: Name one thing you could *taste* in your mouth during that time.

This could be a food you ate just before the session, a drink, or chewing gum. It could be another person or thing if they invaded your space or mouth. As an example, in a car accident, I distinctly remember the taste of metal in my mouth as if I had eaten aluminum foil. When you sit with this idea of which tastes you were able to identify, the scene becomes more present.

____

What was the story that the carrot shared with you?

____

What carrot presented itself to you when you meditated on the concept of guilt?

____

Where was that carrot located in the body?

____

How did it show itself to you?

____

How was it different (if it was different) from the story that you identify with in that particular circumstance?

____

Did you learn anything from what the carrot had to share with you?

____

Circle the color you chose to replace the carrot with and discuss why that color came to your mind.

You can reference the chart at the end of Section I to see what each color signifies.

RED ORANGE YELLOW GREEN BLUE PURPLE WHITE

What name did you give to the carrot for this story?

____

How do you feel in your body after removing the carrot from its rooted place?

____

Affirmation: *Create a simple affirmation to help enforce that it is safe for you to heal.*

____

____

Example affirmations: *It is safe for me to explore the messages of my body.*

I trust the messages of my body.

It is within my own power to heal and release feelings of guilt now.

Pairing the Affirmation with a Hand Position or Mudra

When we create an affirmation to repeat following our deep meditation work, it is important that we also pair the practice with a specific touch to our body to fully activate and align both the tissue memory patterns and the mental groove sets. There are many options to help us dialogue deeply with the body. Feel free to explore all these suggestions and choose the one that works best for you and your specific work.

The two-hand touch involves placing the left middle fingertip directly over your navel. The left hand is the receiving hand. In Chinese medicine this is the CV8 point. The CV8 translates to the "spirit gate." This is a point of integration to help recalibrate your current energy to match the vibrational remedy that is placed upon it.[12]

Place the tip of your right middle finger at the very top of your head at the midline. The right hand is considered the giving hand. This point in Chinese medicine is known as the *baijiu* or the DU20 point. This point translates to "the meeting of the hundreds." It is the place where all the energies within the body converge and meet.[13]

An affirmation you can say while holding the hands in the two positions is: "I am healthy, and I am safe." A more detailed affirmation might be needed according to the work that you have just completed. The affirmation you choose is entirely up to you.

Prayer hands is the most notable hand position or mudra known worldwide to prepare and activate our connection to the heavens as well as to activate the clearing of the mind and the opening of the heart space. Prayer hands asks that God enter our work and help us to clear and heal.

Mudras include touching together specific fingers to activate a certain energy and intention. The most basic hand mudra besides prayer hands is to connect the first finger to the thumb (chin mudra) to connect yourself with the universe. It is a gesture of consciousness. The index finger represents you, and the thumb represents the universe. How you naturally place the two fingers together can give insight into where you are in relation with the universe. If you tuck

the finger under the thumb, this indicates that you are bowing down to the universe. Meeting tip to tip would indicate that you feel even with the universe: not above or beneath the energy itself.

This is ultimately your practice. When creating an affirmation, choose any of these to confirm the dialogue within the body.

Chapter 4
Grief

Grief is an emotion that comes only with tremendous life-changing loss. Grief changes the entirety of the wiring within your system and within the tissues themselves. We are not the same people who we were before grief took us down to the ground. So many times in healing, we want to recover to a place that we can remember before grief entered. Unfortunately, the reality is that this place no longer exists in time. We cannot be the people we were before; it is simply not possible. But we can create something stronger along with that permanent scar. Just as we noted when discussing the art of *kintsugi*, this is the best way to view the healing of grief around yourself.

Grief is not something that we necessarily release, but we can use it as the foundation to rebuild something that weaves the experience and the broken pieces within us into a visible scar of beauty instead of secret pain. Whatever happened in your life that produced the grief, it generally means that something or someone you loved is no longer available to you in life. This might entail an unspeakable tragedy where you are no longer available to yourself in the way you were before. When we think of grief, we tend to think of the loss of someone or something. It can also very easily be the loss of your own self. Grief is a level of despair that is in a class all its own. Some people leave a life-size hole inside us, and that doesn't go away with this type of work.

Grief begins to change all the timelines in our lives. We now live a parallel life; the life we are living in reality, and the life that we might be living if that situation were different. If we lost a person we loved dearly, we count how old they would be now and how different our lives would be with them still in it. Lots of people, once grief strikes, choose to step out of their lives and begin living a false reality within an imaginary space, holding tight to all the things they would be doing if that person or situation were still here. Grief is such a powerful and heartbreaking emotion. No one has any right to tell you how to grieve or for how long. In some ways, we will always grieve. In other ways, there are avenues to gain an opportunity to rebuild.

When it comes to grief, you must learn to sit inside the pain for as long as you need to sit with it. This means not sitting next to your pain, but actually right on the direct flames of the pain. There is no going around grief. The only way to get through it is to go directly through it and feel all of it over and over until you are ready to make small changes that lead to bigger shifts.

I remember going to someone for counseling after my dad passed away. I did not choose therapy for many years following his death. I remember the counselor asking me to tell them one positive thing that came from his death. I thought then and still feel now that this was an incredibly insensitive idea to place on anyone who is grief-stricken. I wasn't there yet, and it's not wise to try to rush anyone through their own process of grieving. Not everything comes with a silver lining. The *glass-half-full* people would argue that everything comes with a silver lining. The *glass-half-empty* side says, how can there be anything positive in losing someone we loved the most in the world? The *I'm just grateful to have a glass at all* people would argue how very blessed we were to have had anyone who loved us so much even though our time was cut short. I think when it comes to navigating grief, it's perfectly okay to be all the above: the glass half-empty, half-full, and grateful for the glass at all. Those are really just stages of learning how to live with grief.

When it comes to grief inside our bodies, it's not for me to say one way or the other how you ought to look at your situations of grief. When you do your meditations and listen carefully to the carrots planted, they can tell you their stories and what they want from you in order to help yourself heal. It's your story to tell and your healing to be offered.

Meditation Tips

Be sure to use the bathroom before beginning this practice. Each practice will take approximately15 to 20 minutes to complete. Lie down in a place where you will be comfortable and not distracted. Turn down the lights, preferably having only natural light in the room. Lie down either on the floor, a couch, or a bed. If you prefer to be seated, this works as well. Be sure you are wearing nonrestrictive clothing.

Relax every part of the external body. Then relax deeper into the organs through auto-suggestion and begin the process of doing the body scan and working with each individual carrot that presents itself for removal, replacing it with something far more loving. Keep in mind that we only work with one carrot per meditation practice. I encourage you to return to the same meditation over and over until you feel that you have cleared every carrot in your body that was planted from this one body emotion before moving on to the next set of somatic emotions. You can fill out the journal and mark on the body as you repeat each practice.

Once you remove the carrot, choose a bucket of hot liquid and also choose the color you wish to use as you fill the space with healthy material. Do not put much thought into what color you will pick for what area. Allow that to come to you naturally. Once you are finished with the meditation you will document where you found this particular carrot in your body and the name that you gave that carrot as well as your color choice. From there, you can look up what color resonates with that area of the body or what that color represents in terms of healing. Remember to go to www.emilyafrancisbooks.com and click on the audio link to receive the meditation.

Audio and Written Meditation

Allow your legs to relax and your feet to fall naturally to each side. Bring your arms out slightly from the body and have the palms facing up. Allow your arms and your legs to be far enough from the center line of your body that they can comfortably lie straight without tension. Allow your arms and legs to hang like the limbs of a rag doll. Notice that they are beginning to feel heavy and limp. Feel your spine lengthen and roll itself out long against the surface beneath you. Gently turn your head from side to side, trying to touch each ear to the surface beneath you, and then settle comfortably in the middle. Exhale all the breath from your body first. Then, gently take a slow, comfortable, full breath in through the nose, and exhale completely through the mouth. Make the sound *ahhhh* on the first deep exhalation to signal to the nervous system that it is time to relax and let go. Breathe in, 1 . . . 2 . . . 3 . . . 4 . . . Hold the breath without tension in your body. Exhale, 1 . . . 2 . . . 3 . . . 4 . . . 5 . . . 6 . . . 7 . . . 8 . . . Hold that space, having your breath fully released before inhaling again. Inhale, 1 . . . 2 . . . 3 . . . 4 . . . Hold the breath in without tension. Slowly and gently exhale 1 . . . 2 . . . 3 . . . 4 . . . 5 . . . 6 . . . 7 . . . 8 . . . and again hold that space before inhaling. Keep this pace as you allow your breath to set the tone for your relaxation. Do not let your breath make you feel anxious, but instead use your breath to guide your body into letting go.

Begin with your feet and tighten them by pointing and flexing them up and down slowly to the rhythm of your breath. Then, relax your feet. Relax your shins and calf muscles. Allow your knees to soften. Feel the tops of your thighs and the back sides of your legs relax. Inhale and hold your breath. Tighten every part of the legs and feet and lift your feet one inch off the surface beneath you. Exhale and allow your legs and feet to drop. Slowly inhale and clench your buttocks, then lift your buttocks and hips off the surface beneath you. Hold your breath as you lift up and tighten the muscles. Exhale, and slowly lower down and tuck your hips under you, allowing your lower back to lie flat on the surface beneath you. Inhale and hold your breath, arch your back, and lift your entire middle and upper back off the surface beneath you. Exhale and slowly lower down. Inhale and lift your shoulders up toward your ears. Hold your breath as your shoulders are raised toward your ears. Exhale and lower your shoulders down. Inhale and hold the breath. Tighten your arms and make a fist with your hands. Lift your arms and hands one inch off the surface beneath you. Exhale and feel the heat and heaviness unwind from the tops of your shoulders, down your upper arms, around the elbows, the forearms and wrists, into the palms of your hands, and off each fingertip as you lower your arms down and relax your hands and each finger. Wiggle your fingers and then relax the entire hand. Inhale and hold your breath. Squeeze your face, tighten your eyelids, and clench your jaw. Exhale and relax your face. Inhale and hold your breath for a moment. Exhale, open your mouth, stick your tongue out as far as you can while making the *ahhh* sound as you open your eyes wide and try to bring the eyebrows up to the top of the hairline. Relax your face and close your eyes comfortably. Relax your jaw and your lips. Rest your tongue gently, either at the roof of your mouth or the bottom of your mouth. Feel your ears soften, your cheeks relax, your chin relax. Relax your eyebrows and forehead. Relax your nose and your nostrils. Relax your scalp and every hair on your head. Breathe slowly and deeply without pressure. Gently bring your awareness all the way up and down your entire physical body, making sure that every part of your body is completely and utterly relaxed.

Allow your mind only to wander deeper into your body now. Going through the organs of the body, we will use an auto-suggestion to relax our organs. Repeat in your mind after me:

Relax my physical body. My body is relaxing. My body is relaxed.

Relax my bladder. My bladder is relaxing. My bladder is relaxed.

Relax my reproductive organs. My reproductive organs are relaxing. My reproductive organs are relaxed.

Relax my small and large intestines. My intestines are relaxing. My intestines are relaxed.

Relax my stomach and pancreas. My stomach and pancreas are relaxing. My stomach and pancreas are relaxed.

Relax my spleen. My spleen is relaxing. My spleen is relaxed.

Relax my liver and gallbladder. My liver and gallbladder are relaxing. My liver and gallbladder are relaxed.

Relax my kidneys and adrenal glands. My kidneys and adrenal glands are relaxing. My kidneys and adrenal glands are relaxed.

Relax my lungs. My lungs are relaxing. My lungs are relaxed.

Relax my heart. My heart is relaxing. My heart is relaxed.

Relax my brain. My brain is relaxing. My brain is relaxed.

Relax all the organs in my body. All my organs are relaxing. All my organs are relaxed.

Relax my mind. I am slowing down my thoughts. I am calming down my feelings. My mind is deeply and completely relaxed.

Relax my entire body. My entire body is relaxing. My entire body is relaxed.

Now bring your awareness into the deepest, darkest, most hidden parts of your body. Go into the bloodstream now and gently surf through your body, through the blood and plasma. Use this liquid flow to guide you throughout your entire body one full time. Become an observer of the way in which your body flows beneath the surface. Bring yourself into the darkness where the master factory of the muscles, fasciae, and other soft tissues are working to keep you alive and healthy. Once you have scanned and surfed through your own flow of movement within, allow your vision to turn inside and go anywhere that your body asks you to go. We begin to scan the entire body all the way from the top of the head to the bottoms of the feet. Go deeper into the layer that is almost never seen, into your sacred garden. All we can see is deep, dark soil laid out through every channel of our body. This is the deepest layer of our being, where only the garden lives. Look for the rows of carrots. Look closely as you begin to notice the greenery of very small carrot tops just above the surface. Discover your garden however you like, whether by walking slowly up and down the lines of the soil, scanning only through your eyes, or gently moving your hands across the body soil in search of green bunches from the tops of the carrots. It is your practice and your choice on how to connect deeply into the spaces where you have planted your harvest. We set our intentions in this deep space that our body opens up to us and unites with our consciousness.

Think of the word ***grief***. We now open ourselves up to any messages, images, or flashes of light or color that catch our eyes and direct them to what comes with the thought of *grief*. Notice that when that word enters your consciousness, one flash will light up from somewhere deep inside your garden. Look for the green leafy top of the carrot that has alerted you to its presence. Bring all your awareness to this one carrot. Imagine a tiny version of yourself coming next to this carrot and sitting down beside it. None of this should be approached quickly. Each carrot has planted itself into the area and grown deep roots from the time of its inception. Be gentle as you look, listen, and ask this carrot to tell you how it got there. Allow the carrot that represents this particular *grief* to tell you its story. Allow this little carrot with deep roots to share its story with you. Your job in this moment is to do nothing but be willing to listen to it and connect with it. No judgment. No opinions. Just be open to hear what it has to tell you.

Once it shares with you an image or an actual story, feel free to give that carrot a name. Name it something to ensure that its story is heard, and that you understand its meaning. Ask the carrot, by its new name, if it would be all right if you pulled it out from the roots and filled the empty area with something soothing, healing, and more loving. Explain to the carrot that it is no longer helpful for it to live there and that you can have great healing if you can move it someplace outside this body. Let that carrot know that this is to help your body come alive into radiant health. Remind the carrot that its story has value and you honor this moment and appreciate that it was so willing to share itself and be vulnerable with you. Once you feel it is safe and that the carrot has given you permission to pull it out from the deep roots, see yourself taking one hand and placing your palm tightly around the bunch as close to the carrot itself as you can get. Gently, but with strong intention, pull the entire carrot out of its place from deep within your garden. Be sure all the roots come out with it. Take a moment to really evaluate the size, shape, and feeling of the hole that remains in its place. Take a few deep breaths and then, with your other hand, choose a bucket of hot liquid to fill this raw, open space quickly and fully. Choose from red, orange, yellow, green, blue, purple, or white. Whatever color you choose is entirely your choice. Pour the bucket's contents into the open space. Watch how quickly the liquid hardens into an opaque crystallized material that radiates its color and its light throughout your entire body. Notice that immediately, the cells from just below where the roots were have begun to light up with the opaque color and move with a whole new vibration. Place a single word of intention into this area to grow and radiate out into your body. Affirm that this intention will now grow and heal inside you. Trust the offering that you just gave to yourself. In this moment of time and space, accept your full permission to heal.

Breathe deeply into this space and when you are ready, take your awareness, still holding the carrot that you removed in your hand, and bring your thoughts up a few layers with the breath until you can feel the air on your skin. In your mind, take the carrot that you removed from the garden and discard it as you see fit. Don't eat it. Plant it in a new garden outside yourself or leave it outside not planted as an offering to the animals. Create a scenario where that carrot that was so full of *grief* is recycled and used for something more positive someplace outside you. Breathe slowly and deeply and keep your eyes closed until the very end. Externalize your awareness and feel the air becoming cooler with each breath. Feel the air around your nostrils and on your skin. Bring yourself back into the room. Gently wiggle your fingers and toes. Lift your arms up and overhead and push your heels away. Stretch and lengthen your entire body. When you are ready, open your eyes and return, return, return.

Journal

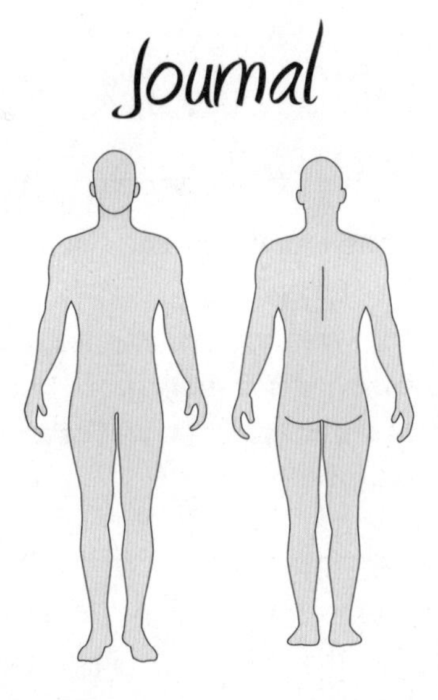

Mark an X where your body was holding the carrot.

Grief Q&A

5-4-3-2-1 Sensory Practice for Grief

Since we can't assume how our brains encode our various experiences, we want to go deep into the scene that our body just showed us. This will help bring it into clear vision in order to disconnect the language loop that our brain and mind have been telling us. Fill in these sensory answers before going directly into the grief experience that your body just shared with you in order to bring it all into the present. We will do a 5-4-3-2-1 practice to gain information from each sensory perception of the experience.

Visual aspect: Name five things that you can *see* in the scene your body showed you.

Look around the space. What can you see? Be very specific.

1 ____

2 ____

3 ______________________________

4 ______________________________

5 ______________________________

Tactile aspect: Name four things you could *touch* in that space.

This includes yourself, what you are sitting, standing, or lying on, maybe the clothes you were wearing, or someone else if they were present. You could list them as well as anything nearby in your memory of the space.

1 ______________________________

2 ______________________________

3 ______________________________

4 ______________________________

Auditory aspect: Name three things you can *hear* in that space.

This could be your voice, someone else's voice, music in the background, or sounds outside your space. Tune in deeply to what sounds are around you in the space your body showed you.

1 ______________________________

2 ______________________________

3 ______________________________

Olfactory aspect: Name two things you can *smell* in that space.

If you were outside or inside, what was around you that you can identify with a scent?

1 ______________________________

2 ______________________________

Gustatory aspect: Name one thing you could *taste* in your mouth during that time.
This could be a food you ate just before the session, a drink, or chewing gum. It could be another person or thing if they invaded your space or mouth. As an example, in a car accident, I distinctly remember the taste of metal in my mouth as if I had eaten aluminum foil. When you sit with this idea of which tastes you were able to identify, the scene becomes more present.

____

What was the story that the carrot shared with you?

____

What carrot presented itself to you when you meditated on the concept of grief?

____

Where was that carrot located in the body?

____

How did it show itself to you?

____

How was it different from the story that you identify with in that particular circumstance?

____

Did you learn anything from what the carrot had to share with you?

____

Circle the color you chose to replace the carrot with and discuss why that color came to your mind.

You can reference the chart at the end of Section I to see what each color signifies.

RED ORANGE YELLOW GREEN BLUE PURPLE WHITE

What name did you give to the carrot for this story?

____

How do you feel in your body after removing the carrot from its rooted place?

____

Affirmation: Create a simple affirmation to help enforce that it is safe for you to heal.

____

____

Example affirmations: *It is safe for me to explore the messages of my body.*

I trust the messages of my body.

It is within my own power to heal and lessen the feelings of grief now.

Pairing the Affirmation with a Hand Position or Mudra

When we create an affirmation to repeat following our deep meditation work, it is important that we also pair the practice with a specific touch to our body to fully activate and align both the tissue memory patterns and the mental groove sets. There are many options to help us dialogue deeply with the body. Feel free to explore all these suggestions and choose the one that works best for you and your specific work.

The two-hand touch involves placing the left middle fingertip directly over your navel. The left hand is the receiving hand. In Chinese medicine this is the CV8 point. The CV8 translates to the "spirit gate." This is a point of integration to help recalibrate your current energy to match the vibrational remedy that is placed upon it.[12]

Place the tip of your right middle finger at the very top of your head at the midline. The right hand is considered the giving hand. This point in Chinese medicine is known as the *baijiu* or the DU20 point. This point translates to "the meeting of the hundreds." It is the place where all the energies within the body converge and meet.[13]

An affirmation you can say while holding the hands in the two positions is "I am healthy and I am safe." A more detailed affirmation might be needed according to the work that you have just completed. The affirmation you choose is entirely up to you.

Prayer hands is the most notable hand position or mudra known worldwide to prepare and activate our connection to the heavens as well as to activate the clearing of the mind and the opening of the heart space. Prayer hands asks that God enter our work and help us to clear and heal.

Mudras include touching together specific fingers to activate a certain energy and intention. The most basic hand mudra besides prayer hands is to connect the first finger to the thumb (chin mudra) to connect yourself with the universe. It is a gesture of consciousness. The index finger represents you, and the thumb represents the universe. How you naturally place the two fingers together can give insight into where you are in relation with the universe. If you tuck

the finger under the thumb, this indicates that you are bowing down to the universe. Meeting tip to tip would indicate that you feel even with the universe, not above or beneath the energy itself.

This is ultimately your practice. When creating an affirmation, choose any of these to confirm the dialogue within the body.

Color Chart

The colors represent a myriad of different ideas. For the purpose of this book, I will list colors according to the energetic stations of the body for healing. However, the color that you use in practice is really your own choice.

- Red: Earth, material attachments, vibrancy, vitality, blood
- Orange: sexual energy, creativity, infusion, fantasy
- Yellow: instinct, trust, knowing or believing, depression, or happiness depending on brightness
- Green: healing, trusting, Earth/nature, loving
- Blue: communication, truth, trust, water
- Purple: regal status, loyalty, healing, creativity, sensuality
- White: spirituality, faithfulness, purity, trust, cleanliness, healing

Section II

The Action Bridge

Suppress, Process, Release

These three chapters will include more action in your meditation and journaling. These meditations and behaviors are required to be put directly into action to create change within your body. Under the suppression of emotion, the body, the mind, or both are trying to take the action of submission and avoidance. If you do not make a decision to heal, you are still making a decision; it's just not a positive one. You can pretend all day long that none of it matters, that you've blindly accepted your past and let go of it in an attempt to not identify yourself through it, but that is BS and somewhere deep inside, you know it. The point of this work is to bring it up from the space of the deep truth that your body has to share and then learn to sit with it, feel it, and to act from out of that space. You can remove, replace, release, and replant.

The purpose of this work is not to make you become delusional about the past. It's also not meant to make you repeat it over and over. My intention is to help you bring it back up through the specific lens of the body so you do not have to do that again moving forward. It's to make peace with the part of the past that involves you specifically and how it has affected your body's internal messaging system. It's the practice of seeing things through the most honest eyes possible and then finding a way to forgive the role that you had to play for whatever reason. For example, it might be a situation where you were too young and didn't know how to find a safe place at the time, or you had zero choice in the matter and things were done without your consent or your control. Self-forgiveness is a necessity in those scenarios. There are real situations where you were 100 percent the victim, and you need to face them and forgive.

There might also be situations when you were not at all the victim but you've played the victim role anyway. It might be that you were involved in the military, served during wartime, and saw things that would make anyone want to jump out of their skin and get out of this life. You might have a situation where you played the role of the violator to other people or animals. I don't know what your story is. I do know that everybody has one. Finding a place of peace with the really rough parts of your story is excruciating because you have to visit them again, but it's necessary to do this work with your body to change the narrative once and for all.

The Difference Between Reexperiencing the Trauma and Feeling Your Feelings

The idea behind this work in particular is not to go all the way back in and relive the experience over again as you were, but instead to watch the experience from the role of the narrator or the observer, not the lead character. Our past traumas do not require us to go down into the grip of the fires again for the actual experience. This is where the work we are attempting to do is different from experiencing the traumas themselves again. This work does ask that we be willing to sit with all the emotions that came from the experience that we just witnessed as the observer. This is the difference with this work. We are exploring the pain that was left inside us from those traumatic experiences. We do not have to live those again in order to heal. We need to work with our bodies and allow them to tell us their stories, and we need to be able to sit with our body experiences and our feelings within them. It is important that we understand that those things are different. Watch as each carrot that has a supporting role inside your body shows you the movie or shares with you how they feel. You do not have to experience the actual traumatic acts again. What I am asking of you is to be willing to experience once and for all the emotions that you've been stuffing down from these experiences.

To change the dynamics of specific body pains, shame, guilt, trauma, and so on, we must be willing to be fully present to the feelings that come with them. The excruciating part of it all is staying still as the discomforts arise and not running away from them any longer. There is no need to make yourself relive the trauma as if you were back in that space, as that only compounds everything down deeper. We need to create an avenue that allows the thoughts and feelings to pass and escape from body tissues. Do your best to watch the old stories, but don't be in them. Be willing to accept the role of the lead character again when it comes to the actual feeling of how it affected you and was planted within the tissues of your body. If you suffer chronic pain, inflammation, phantom pains, nightmares, flashbacks, or anything else residual from those traumatizing experiences, I ask that you be willing to sit with the feelings you've been avoiding.

The goal is to get to the point where you learn to accept the situation as it actually occurred, without your narrative around it, *which is best told by the body itself*. Then you are faced with three possible action practices to make it livable and breathable. The three actions offered are to:

1. Remove and replace, as we did in the previous meditations with the carrots. We pull them out and then replace the hole with something comforting and healing.
2. Remove and release, which is a practice where we go into the image and information that our body provides to us and

then practice a cord-cutting technique to release any other participants who initiated the trauma inflicted on us or on whom we inflicted trauma.

3. Remain and replant. This option allows the carrot to remain in its place, because it has sprouted flowers that hold experiences that make you feel good (which live on the other side of the heavy four). We replant the blossoms to multiply the healthy, healing goodness these blooms bring.

Chapter 5
Suppress

To suppress emotion implies that you have chosen not to revisit the secrets your body has been keeping. It's a choice not to heal and, in effect, remain stagnant in your life. Under this tight holding pattern live anxiety, depression, spite, jealousy, resentment, fear (great amounts of fear), and an unwillingness to see all the wonderful characteristics that you possess. It is a strong desire to stay broken and live in a space of denial.

If you are reading this book, you are now choosing to do the work to heal and shift. Healing is an action behavior. We are never *healed*. We heal certain aspects, and we learn how to use those tools to deal with whatever else crops up in our lives that we need to heal. But life is life! Even if we've cleared and healed everything in our past, at a point in the present, rest assured, you will face hard times again that will create new problems (although they can trigger the old ones as well), and you will need to apply this same wisdom and work with the new patterns that come up with being human and loving others around us. Life will kick our asses, be assured. It's how we navigate those tough times that counts. Now that we are learning how our bodies take it all on, it's more important than ever to never leave our bodies behind as we pull ourselves back up and try to move on after difficulties and tragedies.

Chronic Emotions Versus Acute Emotions

Some people are plagued by a chronic level of depression or anxiety. The brain has rewired to function at this capacity. Until both the brain and the mind are treated, it will be nearly impossible to change the tracks. Understand that the brain is an organ. It is where the neurotransmitters live, the synapses, the chemicals, and the highway system of the nerves to communicate with the entire body. The mind is not of that nature. The mind is where the thoughts live. The mind is where experiences are felt and processed. This is why when our brains get out of balance, it is wise to consult with a psychiatrist (a doctor who tests and diagnoses issues and then prescribes therapy, medication, or herbs) to help rewire the chemical imbalance that has occurred in the brain. At the same time, seeing a psychologist, psychotherapist, talk therapist, hypnotherapist, or counselor who works specifically with how we understand, react, process, and navigate our behavior patterns is ideal. The mind deals with how we think and feel. The brain deals with how we function based on how we think and feel.

Entirely too many people on this planet are walking shells of themselves. Depression and anxiety plague the human culture all around the world. If you are experiencing either of these emotions, you must first figure out if it is something chronic or something directly associated with where you currently are in your life. For instance, if you are going through a loss, a divorce, a move, or a change in career, it is reasonable to feel completely overwhelmed with anxiety or depression depending on the chemical make up of your body. I remember when my friend was going through her divorce, she said every morning she would wake up, roll over, look at the ceiling, and say, "Shit. Not again." She did not want to be here, but she would never consider ending her life on her own. She just wished it would happen for her. I'm now hearing more and more stories about people who go to bed at night praying that they don't wake up in the morning. These are considered manic episodes, highly acute (I hope), and you must get true professional help immediately. If you are experiencing such episodes, put this book down and come back to your work after you've seen a professional who can help regulate what is happening with your brain and mind.

Now, in thinking about something more long-term or chronic, we must figure out when this started and how. We have our obvious assumptions of when it all began, but remember that the body may have a very different story and timelines in place. Do not direct the body under your assumptions. Go in with an open mind and allow the body to guide you to where the carrots are buried and show you what specific scenarios they pair with. This is again a deep, internal body scan that requires you to locate the carrot that planted itself into your internal tracking system. Once we pinpoint that time during our lives, we must not only remove the carrot, and fill the empty space with something much more healing and affirming, but we may also wish to put into practice the release techniques so that we can cut once and for all the cords that may bind us to others who inflicted the heavy pains. We also have to do the deep dive into the actual scenario. We have to be willing to put ourselves back into it (again as the narrator, not the lead role). Begin this meditation and scan the body for when your depression or anxiety set itself only when you are strong enough to go back and sit with your feelings for the moment.

For this action section, I am challenging you to sit directly inside your feelings. You won't get to change the story. You will only be allowed to change the way you handle it on the inside going forward. This will open you to the opportunity to reset the dialogue and deal with the self-deprecation that you've been engaging in since that moment in time. You must be willing to ask yourself and answer honestly whether you are ready to take that dive in. If the answer is yes, then let's go into the work. If it's not yes today, that is perfectly okay. Every day ask yourself the question until the answer changes. Ask this question: *Am I willing to go back into my stories exactly how they happened, and be willing to listen to what my body has to say, and feel how my body truly experienced those feelings*?

Notice that deciding before the actual meditation work which story we are going into in order to determine where the actual planting of the carrot occurred within our bodies says that our minds have made up what story goes with what pain. When we learn to listen only to the body and its interpretation of pain and the origin of its creation, they very well might not be the same story at all. It might be a different situation that set the body off. This makes it very difficult because not only am I asking you to sit through and replay in your movie-screen mind what you perceive as your worst situations, but I am also asking you to be willing to sit through the stories and movie screens from inside the body, and those stories might be something else entirely. The story that you have always applied to the specific time marker as associated with anxiety or depression might not be the same story as when your body began to feel it. Every time you enter this meditation, you must be open to what your body has to say and do not attempt to speak for it. The body is full of magic and wisdom. *Today, are you ready to allow it to speak?*

The Somatic Languages

The body uses certain behaviors to communicate. Let's take a side step and match up the communicating language of the body that we can all understand and trace the deeper meanings. I call these the five somatic languages of the body. These languages are the result of combined study of the body as well as my own personal observances of the body.

1. Laughing
2. Crying
3. Yelling
4. Running or hiding
5. Bowel disturbances

Looking into Each of the Five Somatic Languages

There are different ways that the body expresses its feelings.

Laughing: Could be out of pure happiness and freedom. That kind of laughter comes from deep in the belly. True and authentic enjoyment for the present moment can produce the greatest kind of laughter. When we consider the other side, however, ask if you are someone who laughs in response to other people's pain. If someone falls down, do you laugh? Has your laughter caused someone hurt recently? Is it a nervous response?

Emerging research on the physiology of laughter has increased steadily over the years, along with practices such as laughter yoga. There are five identified separate types of laughter: genuine ("spontaneous"), self-induced ("simulated"), stimulated (e.g., tickling), induced (e.g., via drugs), and pathological. There are many health benefits to laughter, whether it is induced by watching something humorous or is spontaneous laughter. In this research, it was found that "52 patients show[ed] a 1-hour humor video found increases in natural killer cell activity, IgG, IgM, and other leukocytes and another study of 20 subjects found that an amusing film actually produced similar increases in epinephrine and norepinephrine levels."[14]

Crying: Do you cry because you are so happy that no other emotion can express the deep sense of joy and gratitude that you are feeling? Or do you cry because you are so frustrated and so upset that there are simply no words to be used? Tears spill from the corner of the eyes and sting as they make their way down your face. Do you tend to cry when you are sad? Those are the salty tears. Many people stick their tongue out to taste the sad tears that always seem to gravitate to the corners of the mouth.

There are three confirmed types of tears: basal tears, which are always in the eyes to protect from outside debris and for lubrication; reflex tears, which might occur due to irritants such as smoke and cutting into onions; and emotional tears, which are produced when we feel sadness, happiness, or other intense emotions.[15] In her research, the famed Rose Lynn-Fischer found that grief tears were completely different structures than, say, an onion tear or even a sad tear. She says: "Tears are the medium of our most primal language in moments as unrelenting as death, as basic as hunger and as complex as a rite of passage." She goes on to say, "It's as though each one of our tears carries a microcosm of the collective human experience, like one drop of an ocean." She also says, "Emotional tears, for instance, have been found to contain protein-based hormones including the neurotransmitter leucine enkephalin, a natural painkiller that is released when the body is under stress."[16]

Yelling: Are you a natural yeller? Have you always been a yeller? Is this a trait you have taken on from your family or loved ones? Do you yell when you are angry? Do you yell when you are happy and need to shout out loud? Do you yell when you don't feel like you are being heard or validated? "Being frequently yelled at changes the mind, brain and body in a multitude of ways including increasing the *activity of the amygdala* (the emotional brain), *increasing stress hormones* in the blood stream, increasing muscular tension and more."[17] This is the description of what being yelled at might do to our bodies. But what is the physiological occurrence happening within our bodies when we are doing all the yelling? Research shows that when we yell, "our brain can be split into two parts: the emotional part (the limbic system) and the logical part (the cerebral cortex). This is usually what is famously the left-brain versus right-brain explanation. Anger is predominantly felt in the limbic center, and the person stops using the cerebral cortex for experiencing and expressing anger." It goes on to say that "when we get angry, the heart rate, arterial tension and testosterone production increases, cortisol (the stress hormone) decreases, and the left hemisphere of the brain becomes more stimulated. This is indicated by a new investigation led by scientists from the University of Valencia . . . that analyzes the changes in the brain's cardiovascular, hormonal, and asymmetric activation response when we get angry. Note that this study was carried out on 30 males, so it may be gender biased."[18]

Running or hiding: Are you someone who runs when things become too overwhelming? Do you find that you just have to get away to collect yourself when things are too much for you? Do you run away from confrontation? Do you like to be invisible in certain situations? Do you prefer the role of the observer rather than someone involved in any given situation? Is hiding your go-to method of coping?

Here is what the research demonstrates about fight, flight, running, hiding, or withdrawal. The psychological responses are these: the stress response begins in the brain (in the amygdala where messages are interpreted), sending a distress signal to the hypothalamus (where it communicates to the whole body and signals to the autonomic nervous system to put on their flight gear). Next the adrenal glands sound their bell and release hormones (adrenaline most notably). All this occurs before the body can even process what is happening with the eyes. The body acts before the mind can catch up to what is happening. The physiological response (what happens in the body) includes a fast heartbeat, high amounts of short breaths, increases in blood pressure and blood sugar, sweating, tense muscle activity, and a decrease in digestion. Even if you get nervous bowels, you will not defecate while running and hiding.[19]

Bowel disturbances: This is a big one that you need to pay attention to. Do your bowels indicate where you are in your life? Do you tend to get constipated? Are you regular? Are your bowels healthy and not loose? Do you go more than once a day or even daily at all? Can you match your emotions to your bowel movements? I remember before a big sports competition I felt like I had to run to the bathroom with fairly explosive bowels. My friend told me her family calls them the *nervous poopies*. I still refer to them as such to this day. If you are about to do something scary or challenging, do you suddenly have to run to the bathroom? If you become angry or extremely upset, do you have to use the bathroom often, or not at all? These are real physiological body languages that match up with your current emotions. You must pay attention to them. Science and society are finally catching on to the mind/brain/gut connection, hallelujah!

It is a documented fact that "anxiety changes the gut function."[20] But anxiety isn't the only emotional pattern that affects the way our bowels react. This is why it is now more commonplace for doctors to prescribe antianxiety and antidepressant medication to treat bowel disorders such as irritable bowel syndrome. More research has emerged indicating that maybe it's not that our anxiety or depression causes the bowel disturbance, but that it might actually go both ways. Bowel disruptions can also lead us into anxiety or depression. The gut and brain connection is much more massive than we ever used to understand. "In a study in Australia over a twelve-year period, over 1,000 people who had chronic gut issues were followed. Fifty percent had anxiety first. The other fifty percent developed gut disorders before the onset of any psychological problems. In the latter, the researchers are led to believe that it was the gut/brain disorder that led to the increase in anxiety."[20] So what came first, the chicken or the egg? No one knows with certainty. What it does show for the purpose of this work is that our bowels tell a whole heck of a lot about our feelings and the way in which we are able to express and balance those feelings.

Meditation Practice

We will not do a formal meditation for suppression, because we do not want to encourage this behavior. Instead, the meditation for this section will be a hands-on listening practice of your body. This will help you formulate the next steps of the work and bring it all into action.

Meditation for Listening to the Messages of Your Body

In this meditation, I want you to feel as if you are coming to me for a hands-on experience. We are not focusing on actual healing in this meditation. Instead, we are listening to the body tell us where we need to focus our work and beginning to commit to the actions required to cross the bridge. Even though I can work with your body only through this meditation and not with actual touch, it is possible to experience the healing and continue my work through your own hands.

Let's begin.

Clear away any clutter and come into a space where you can lie down on your back comfortably with no distractions. Light candles if possible and dim the lights. Do not have full bright lights on for this practice; only have natural light. Lie down and close your eyes. Exhale all the air and release tension from your body first. Inhale slowly through your nose and hold your breath for a moment before exhaling through your mouth. Inhale through your nose for 1 . . . 2 . . . 3 . . . 4 . . . and hold the breath comfortably. Exhale through the mouth for 1 . . . 2 . . . 3 . . . 4 . . . 5 . . . 6 . . . 7 . . . 8 . . . Inhale slowly through your nose and exhale steadily through the mouth. Set the tone of the breathing as slow, full, and comfortable to the body. Focus on your breath. Feel the air enter against the skin of your nostrils. Feel your stomach expand and rise with each inhale.

Lower your navel down toward your spine with each exhalation. You are in a warm, safe environment for your hands-on healing work. This is a sacred space with no judgment to any reaction your body may have. As I place my hands on you, know that my touch and yours are completely safe, with no expectation of anything in return except clean, pure, unattached touch in order to communicate with your body's muscular, energetic, and emotional system.

Imagine that I now place the palms of my hands gently on the tops of your feet. My hands are warm and confident, offering a safe feeling to the touch. You instinctively know that with my touch, I have no ulterior motive other than healing intended for your greatest and highest good. As my hands are placed on the tops of your feet, I can feel the energy pattern circling through and around your body. Each person has a different energy pattern. Some can feel very fragmented at first, but through the healing work, it becomes one continuous circle of flowing energy surrounding the body. Bring your awareness to the touch of my hands and feel the energy pattern from your feet. Allow your feet to relax and your legs to become heavy and limp.

I now move my hands to the tops of your knees. Your knees govern your ability to move forward in your life. Breathe into the space and feel the warmth of my healing hands lying gently on the tops of your kneecaps. Notice how you feel with any touch on your legs. Do you feel comfortable? Do you feel safe? Listen closely to what your legs are trying to tell you. What is the message of your lower body?

Gently, we move to the area of your hips. My hands will not be on you this time, but rather your own. Place your palms gently on each hip bone. Breathe through your hands and send warmth, safety, and loving touch through your own hands into your hips. Breathe into this space and open your heart and mind to listen to the messages that your body is sending you. Move your hands from your hip bones to the navel. Place one hand over the navel and the other hand on top of that hand. Do not press down on the navel. Simply move your hands with your breath as the navel rises and falls each time you inhale and exhale. Talk to the area of your body that spans from your hip bones, where you just were, to the navel, where you are now. How many messages sit in this particular area of your body? Does your body feel healthy and liberated here? Or is this place holding on to trauma, guilt, shame, heaviness, or secrets or pain of any kind?

Move your hands to your heart center, located in the center of your chest. You can place one hand in the center of the chest with the other hand over it as you did with the navel, or you may place one hand on each side of your chest close to the collar bones. Breathe into your hands and open the palms of your hands to breathe through your hands and send heat into the body. Heat indicates that you are open to receive the energy and messages of the body.

There are so many secrets that we hide close to our hearts. Breathe into this space and allow your hands to follow your breath. What does your heart have to share with you? Let it whisper its secrets and desires into the palms of your hands. Feel your heart space open up with every breath. Allow the heart to experience complete nonjudgmental openness and love coming from the center of your palms. Become silent as you listen deeply to the messages of your heart. Stay here in the silence and simply become fully open and aware. When you are ready, place one hand across your chest to the shoulder and cross your other arm to the other shoulder, like you are giving yourself a hug. Keep the palms of your hands on the tops of your shoulders and breathe deeply and softly into this space.

The shoulders and the arms have much to share with us if we can open ourselves to listen to the wisdom of their messages. Breathe into this space and gently ask your entire upper body for any information that it needs to share with you so you can help it heal. Hold this space and give yourself deep love from this position. Make no judgment; do not let your mind start answering from your body. Allow your body to speak its truth without disruption. Listen intently and do not answer for any part of the internal messaging system.

Now move your hands toward your neck and throat area. Keep your hands slightly above your actual throat, not touching it but close enough to feel the heat from your hands. Try to relax your face as your hands hover over your throat. This, too, is a high-energy and vulnerable area of the body. Things have been spoken and secrets kept. Feelings of being validated and heard throughout the many stages of your life may reside in this area. Ask your throat area to share with you anything you need to know in order to help yourself heal. Stay in this space for several breaths. Get as quiet as you can so you can hear the authentic voice speak its truth to you.

Place your palms over your eyes now. The middle of your palm is directly over the eye socket, not necessarily touching your eyes themselves, but the whole hand is touching the area above and below your actual eye. The heat from your hands can be easily felt in this sensitive area. Breathe into this space and talk to your eyes. The eyes have not only felt everything that has happened in your life, but the eyes have seen it all, too. What do your eyes need you to remember? What do your eyes need you to feel? What do your eyes ask of you in order to help release into healing?

Now inhale slowly and as you exhale, slowly rub your palms down your face and down your chest to the navel. Bend both arms, resting the palms at the navel. Now scan your body through your hands. Is there any place on your body that is begging to have your healing hands? Move your hands to any place within your body, the back side or the front side, that needs to feel the touch of unconditional love, openness, and listening without judgment. Go to the area of your body that calls you there. Stay in that space and try to locate the area. Is it an organ? Is it a muscle? Is it tissue without a name? What does this space hold for you? What does your body need you to hear? Stay in that space for as long as your body asks you to. Please, make the decision now in your heart and mind to accept the challenge of facing, accepting, releasing, and moving into the lighter sides of your experiences. It is time to move out of suppressing any secrets, any pains, and set yourself on the road to release and receive.

Once you feel the movement still, gently bring your arms down by your sides and keep your eyes closed. Breathe slowly and softly and ask that you remember every single experience and message that your body has just given to you. Wiggle your fingers and your toes and bend your knees as you roll to one side. Gently sit up, bring yourself back to the present space, and return, return, return.

Journal

List your behavior patterns in order, from the most-used pattern to the least.

_____ Laughing
_____ Crying
_____ Yelling
_____ Running or hiding
_____ Bowel disturbances

Once you see your order, what thoughts come to you about this? Is anything worth noting?

____

____

What things have you chosen to suppress until this point?

____

____

What messages did your body offer in this practice?

____

____

What can you do with the information your body provided?

____

____

There is no affirmation practice with this section. It is all about listening to your body and gently asking yourself if you are ready to continue with this work.

____

____

____

Chapter 6
Process

The Both/And Approach

The process through which you allow yourself to heal will be so much easier if you adopt the both/and approach to healing as opposed to the either/or way of life. How you choose to process through your body's traumas is really important. If you treat *both* the physical *and* the emotional, you have a higher chance of healing more fully. If you approach life, health, faith, and so on with the both/and approach, you can study both and still find a way to be happy and healthy...but it will cost you in the short run. It goes against the grain of any mainstream standard protocol to a life of health, healing, and everything else. Both/and folks can make people nervous and uncomfortable. It implies that you are open to both and can apply all to the individual areas of your life. It implies that you are a gatherer of information. You tend to be open to all sides and have a natural curiosity to what happens on the other side of what you've known. How do they do it on the other side of the world? While the either/ors have no desire to find out such answers, the both/ands tend to need to know. This goes outside the box that has been designed for you. For this work, I urge you to work under the both/and umbrella. Be open to this work and open to the messages of your own body. Do not dismiss this because it's not as formulated and researched as the original philosophies of the standard approach to healing.

You need this for yourself, or you would not have picked up this particular book. You can tackle the hard things. You can change the dynamics of how your body has held on to traumas. You must be committed and willing to doing the work, and the work is asking you to dive into your body and be open to receiving what it has to say to you. It also asks that you not only listen but also spring into action in a way that you have not yet done before in the name of your healing. You can reclaim any aspect of your life that you might currently think was lost. It's all there for you! As I said before, the caveat is that it will not be easy. It will, however, be worth it. The processing part of this work can be, in my opinion, the most difficult part of this entire deal. Getting through the practices and getting into action will take you to the release, and that is the goal: crossing the action bridge into greatness. Turning back and keeping all the same feelings suppressed will only continue to weigh heavily on you. The processing platform can go either way, one side or the other. Everything from this work will set the tone for how you take ownership of knowing your next right step and then finally taking it. Slow and steady wins this race. Don't push yourself too hard and too fast. This action bridge is daunting. As Dory says in *Finding Nemo*, "Just keep swimming." Just keep taking that next right step, one foot after the other. Don't look back, don't run back to familiar patterns—they didn't work for you. Keep looking forward and let your body lead.

When it comes to the either/or approach to life and healing, it can be tough to work from. I bring this up because how we approach our personal healing is very much based on one of these two approaches, and the both/and as well as the either/or will come up with a consequence on the tail of the action. Every action has a consequence. What we don't realize is that *consequence* does not always have to be a negative term. Doing good things will result in good outcomes. That is still the consequence of your action. It's the if/then idea: "If you do one thing, then this will be the outcome." This occurs following every single thing you do and don't do. They are both actions. Because we are now deep into the action bridge of our somatic approach to healing, the consequences bar has just been elevated to an all-time high. This is your life. You are as young as you will ever be again, and as old as you have ever been. Do not waste another moment of your life sitting in a shit-storm from emotions and experiences that went unexpressed and wreaked havoc on your system. You can heal and become a healthier version of yourself as soon as you make the commitment to do so and follow through on that promise. Process the hell out of this part so we can move on to all the great stuff sitting on the other side and waiting for you to learn with the joy-seeking parts of your life.

Neither approach to life and healing is right or wrong. If you are an either/or person and you are trying to find your way into a deeper, more valuable balance of your inner workings, then this is perfectly acceptable! This is where going to your medical doctors and proper therapists, reading scripture, and following the rules can keep you happy, healthy, and safe. You can still achieve great inner healing by following in the footsteps that have been set out for you. But the approach is different. You might need to visit a clergy member and ask for forgiveness in order to feel healthy and whole. You may or may not choose to face some of the damages that others have done to you or you have done to yourself; these events have created your need to heal in the first place. You may choose to do your own healing and still never say out loud to anyone what you needed to heal from. As long as you focus solely on you, it's not right or wrong to confront, repeat, or protect anyone else. Doing the work with the cord-cutting might be exactly the right next step for you.

Many people say they are open to all forms of healing, but in truth they are usually open only to the healing that is within their comfort zone. We must be willing to answer the questions and face the realities that have been keeping us broken if we want to claim big healing. That takes courage and a willingness to listen with an open mind and an open heart to what your body needs to share with you.

Creating a Healing Environment

An important and sometimes overlooked environmental factor is your current physical location. The environment that you are in is more important than almost any aspect of healing. We have to learn how to create a healthy environment that lives both within us and outside ourselves. This includes how we deal with our truths as they come up, the people who either live with us or are closest to us, and the physical area of the world and culture that we are located in. There are a lot of things that factor in when it comes to our healing and creating a better life for ourselves. This is part of the process of releasing patterns for the life that lies ahead of us. Being in a healthy environment that feeds and nourishes all aspects of your body, your mind, and your soul is paramount to living a healthy and contented life.

The environment is not just the physical place. It can be family members. It can be your spiritual community. Environment in this context means every person, every natural wonder, and the world within yourself and all around you. Being around people who keep you down will never allow you the opportunity to feel truly free and happy. Gaslighters are everywhere if you allow them to be. The act of gaslighting is defined by the *Encyclopedia Britannica* as "an elaborate and insidious technique of deception and psychological manipulation, usually practiced by a single deceiver, or 'gaslighter,' on a single victim over an extended period. Its effect is to gradually undermine the victim's confidence in his own ability to distinguish truth from falsehood, right from wrong, or reality from appearance, thereby rendering him pathologically dependent on the gaslighter in his thinking or feelings."[21]

While growing into your next phase in life, if your life is in a place that stunts growth, you will begin to feel it everywhere. I'm not asking you to move. I am asking you to first begin with this work of listening to your body and honoring its messages, and then, yes, I am asking that you create a ripple effect of change in all areas that surround you in your new level of health and healing. Believe it or not, there are many people out there who do not want you to feel whole and healthy. Some people love to keep us broken. That way, they can still manipulate us. Claiming your whole self in a healthy and balanced way will intimidate many people around you. The ones cheering for you from the back, though? Move those folks up to the front. Those are the people you need to surround yourself with—people who are not attached to your brokenness and take great pleasure in watching you rise and shine brightly.

Astrocartography

Have you ever heard of astrocartography? It's a grid design based on your birth chart of where your soul is highest and lowest according to the geographical location where you live.[22] Whether you subscribe to that doctrine or not, everyone can conceptualize where their happy place is, where they feel totally connected to their own soul. It's a place that makes us feel like the very best version of ourselves. This place exists both within you when you have done the work required to attain true liberation and peace, and also it lives out in the world where you feel yourself come alive. I've come to realize that the environment might not change who you are, but your environment can possibly help you to facilitate your own change into who you are becoming.

There once was a time in my life when all that I was responsible for was myself and my one dog. If I didn't like something, I could literally up and move. You don't like something? Then leave! We see it all the time; we hear things like, "You don't like it, then move. You're not a tree!" Or we see both single people and even families all over social media who have left their jobs to travel the world and make money, posting pictures and doing video montages of their incredible life of freedom and joy. That is the new Instagram life! I will not knock it. I think it's wonderful that social media can now offer an entirely new existence. If you feel called to do that, then I say by all means, go for it all the way! You still have to do your internal work, though, to find your truth, balance, healing, and recovery so you can fully enjoy that new life. You can take this book with you anywhere, listen to the meditations, fill in the journals, and help free yourself internally from pain and extra emotional weight. I am totally on your team for this! Just be sure that the life you are creating is authentic and not suited up for social media. Social media is not necessarily real life. You are being tasked with doing real-life work, and only you can decide what that looks like and where it resides. Becoming *real* is so liberating, and I want that for you. I know all too well what it's like to live life under the guise that we've got it all figured out. The figuring-out part actually comes along the road when you finally own up to the fact that you have not, in fact, gotten any of it figured out. It's in the truth and honesty and the vulnerability of not pretending that we finally get to become what we might have always wanted to be. Please don't get tangled up in seeing other people's highlights on social media platforms and thinking that's what their daily life looks like. Notice how much you gravitate toward the ones that are raw and honest and real with people. If you aspire to become anything, look to be one of those who has cleaned house, done the work, learned to work from the inside, let the skeletons loose, and owned up to the part they play as the lead role of their life. That doesn't come with a location; it comes from inside. That is our goal with this work.

If you are not able to leave your current location or even get away from some of those who have contributed to your pain, then we need to have a different conversation. Some people are caregivers and can't leave. Others are parents of special needs children or any children, and changing their environment can be way too much to put on them. If your family has friends and a life that they love, it's almost impossible to disrupt that, even if you are not happy being there. Some are addicts and can't make big decisions until they change everything within themselves to heal and thrive. Others are living in a place that doesn't resonate with them for a myriad of reasons—financial, family, health, and so on—but can't change that reality in this moment. Everything in life has an ebb and a flow, and what life looks like outside your windows is not what it will look like in a year or two or five. The location can change, and if you do it right, that change of location can be glorious. It can also be a disaster. I left to live with a friend in another state once to help get over a terrible breakup. When I got there, I had a couple of days of bliss with my best friend, but for the rest of the time I lived there, I barely ever saw her. She worked all day and stayed with her boyfriend (now husband) every night. I moved to be close to someone who all but moved out after my arrival. It was lonely and miserable, and I ended up back home after only a short amount of time. One friend referred to it as "my vacation with all my stuff." Changing physical environments without doing any of the internal work did nothing but backfire on my plans.

Many spiritual practices suggest that inner peace offers you sustainability and happiness no matter what the outside looks like. I understand and appreciate the concept, but let's put it in a different context. If you are peaceful but living in a war zone with people being literally slaughtered around you, how do you justify your inner peace? Are you helping anyone or just sitting on your meditation pillow all Zen-like? Is that healing? Your environment matters greatly. Creating the calmest, healthiest, and most positive world for yourself both inside and outside your door is the best way to get through your processing time and into the release.

For the purpose of processing, we must change the order in which we have been approaching our healing. The term *process* is such an umbrella term regarding health. One definition of *healing* is "the process of the restoration of health to an unbalanced, diseased, or damaged organism."[23] It is a *process*. It can basically summarize the entire journey into healing. But *processing,* as I see it, is more the work that is done internally as we learn to work with our body and then rearrange the conversations that it is having to optimize internal health. In the practice of processing, we relive the situations we've been stuffing down for a tremendous amount of time. It's the journey into coming clean with ourselves and anyone that our repressed emotions or life experiences have harmed. For this work, we must fill out the journal and get organized with what our process needs to be before we can do the meditation to clear out what's been holding us back.

A practice I learned many years ago will be the foundation of what I ask of you in the journal ahead. We have two lobes in our brains. Within those lobes, specific areas govern different behaviors and understanding. Without getting too technical, a part of the brain stores our childhood memories in a way that keeps us present to those childhood moments. Remember how I said when there is a trauma, it locks into the brain and freezes in time? We want to get into those frozen pieces and work with them. One way to do this is to use the nondominant hand to write answers to a series of questions written out by the dominant hand. In the journal provided, the questions are already listed so you won't have to think of any.

The practice will be to write each answer down with your nondominant hand. The other part of the practice is not to stop, not to read the answers, and not to judge the answers. Just fill out the journal all the way through and then look at your answers. When we find ourselves saying things like, "What are they talking about? That is messy," or "That didn't happen like that" or any other judgmental thoughts, that is a clear indicator that you have returned to the part of the brain that would be run by your dominant hand. You are back in your adult space. It can be a waste of time and energy to judge it. Also, for this work, please try not to preread the questions. Read them only as you are writing your answers. You may be very surprised by your answers. I certainly was when I did this work for my own processing and healing. It's a quick way to open up the part of the brain that holds our childhood way of thinking.

Journal

Answer the questions below with your nondominant hand.

What is your name?

____

Where do you live?

____

Who do you live with?

____

Where do you go to school?

____

What do you love to eat?

____

What do you love to do?

____

Who are your favorite people?

____

Who are the people you are afraid of?

____

Why?

____

Can you draw a picture of your house?

____

Can you draw a picture of your family?

____

What is your favorite kind of ice cream?

____

Does anyone take you to get ice cream?

____

What is your favorite memory?

____

What is your first memory of being really sad? What happened?

____

____

When was the first time someone hurt you?

____

Who was it? What happened?

____

____

What did you do? Did you tell anyone?

____

____

Did they do it again?

____

Are there any secrets that you have been keeping?

____

Do you feel safe in your home?

____

Do you feel safe at school or work?

____

Is there any place you do not feel safe? Why?

____

____

Where do you feel happiest?

____

You can share anything you want to share here:

____

____

____

____

Now move the pen to the dominant hand and read your answers. Does anything you wrote stick out to you? What is significant from this work?

Other Additions to Note

Getting into the child brain and searching for trauma is only one way that we utilize the processing portion for our internal healing. There are, of course, other ways that we can process, but it really comes down to the action of remembering painful events as they occurred, without letting our judgment and animations get the better of us, and working through anything that has held us back. It can be a process of forgiveness that actually has nothing to do with any other people (meaning we do not need to forgive anyone else in order to forgive the part of ourselves that was affected). It is in the release of the attachment of the part that you played in it. Forgiveness isn't the all-holy practice of playing the martyr. It's about forgiving ourselves for the part we played and releasing the attachments that we have carried toward someone. That, too, is a process.

Remember that it's not about anyone outside yourself for this work. It's about you and your attachment to any and all of it. It's the conversation that your body and your mind have kept (and many times those conversations are not exactly the same) that need to be changed. This comes down to awareness and ownership of your health and healing. The more information you have, the easier it will be to make a permanent decision to change. Taking charge of your body, your health, and your healing is the ultimate goal in this work. It is to finally begin to listen to your body and what it has been trying to say to you. It's learning what it has been holding on to that you might have waved off as insignificant given how much time has passed. You cannot afford to do that anymore if you want to heal yourself from the deep seeds that were planted during those times. This is the art of the process. The process is not pretty, and it should not be something quick. There is no quick fix for years of holding patterns and heartache that you have suffered along the way. It's taken however many years to build into this place you've found yourself living from. It won't get fixed or mended in a week. This is work. The whole purpose of this book is to offer you the chance to process any grief, pain, shame, sorrow, and guilt that you have been carrying around with you that may well be the culprit in any discomforts, illness, or disease you may be dealing with. What I'm asking you to do in this section is to face it and own it and do something to change it. That way, we can move on into all the lighter sides of this book and within your body and discover that you have also been storing some really good stuff in those tissues as well.

Meditation Tips

Be sure to use the bathroom before beginning this practice. Each practice will take approximately 15 to 20 minutes to complete. Lie down in a place where you will be comfortable and not distracted. Turn down the lights, preferably having only natural light in the room. Lie down either on the floor, a couch, or a bed. If you prefer to be seated, this works as well. Be sure you are wearing nonrestrictive clothing.

Relax every part of the external body. Then relax deeper into the organs through auto-suggestion and begin the process of doing the body scan and working with each individual carrot that presents itself to you. Keep in mind that we only work with one carrot per meditation practice. I encourage you to return to the same meditation over and over until you feel that every carrot in your body that was planted from this one body emotion has multiplied as much as possible before moving on to the next set of somatic emotions. You can fill out the journal and mark on the body as you repeat each practice.

Audio and Written Meditation

Allow your legs to relax and your feet to fall out naturally to each side. Bring your arms out slightly from your body and have the palms facing up. Allow your arms and your legs to be far enough from the center line of your body that they can comfortably lie straight. Allow your arms and legs to hang like the limbs of a rag doll. Let your arms and legs begin to feel heavy and limp. Feel your spine straighten and become heavy on the surface beneath you. Roll your head from side to side and then settle comfortably in the middle.

Exhale all the breath from your body first. Then take a slow, comfortable, full breath in through the nose, and exhale completely through the mouth. Make the sound *ahhh* on the first deep exhalation to signal to the nervous system that it is time to relax. Breathe in: 1 . . . 2 . . . 3 . . . 4 . . . Hold the breath without tension in the body. Exhale: 1 . . . 2 . . . 3 . . . 4 . . . 5 . . . 6 . . . 7 . . . 8 . . . Hold that space without the breath before inhaling again. Slow your breathing and allow the breath to set the tone for your relaxation.

Begin with your feet and tighten them by pointing and flexing them up and down slowly to the rhythm of your breath. Relax your feet. Relax your shins and calf muscles. Allow your knees to soften. Feel the tops of your thighs and the back sides of your legs relax. Inhale and hold your breath now. Tighten every part of the legs and feet and lift your feet one inch off the surface beneath you. Exhale and allow your legs and feet to drop. Slowly inhale and clench the buttocks, then lift the buttocks and hips off the surface beneath you. Hold your breath as you lift up and tighten the muscles. Exhale and slowly lower down and tuck the hips under you, allowing the lower back to lie flat on the surface beneath you. Inhale and hold your breath, arch your back, and lift your entire middle and upper back off the surface beneath you. Exhale and slowly lower down. Inhale and lift your shoulders up toward your ears. Hold your breath as your shoulders are raised as high as they can go. Exhale and lower the shoulders down. Inhale and hold the breath. Tighten your arms and make a fist with your hands. Lift your arms and hands one inch off the surface beneath you. Exhale and feel the heat and heaviness unwind from the tops of your shoulders, down your upper arms, around the elbows, the forearms and wrists, into the palms of your hands, and off each fingertip as you lower the arms down and relax the hands. Inhale and hold your breath. Squeeze your face, tighten your eyelids, and clench your jaw. Exhale and relax your face. Inhale and hold your breath for a moment. Exhale and open your mouth, stick your tongue out as far as you can, open your eyes wide, and try to bring your eyebrows up to the top of your hairline. As you stick your tongue out and exhale, make the *ahhh* sound again, signaling to your central nervous system to let go. Once you have released the final audible exhalation, gently relax your entire face. Relax your ears. Relax your scalp and every hair on your head. Breathe slowly and deeply without pressure. Gently bring your awareness all the way up and down your entire physical body, making sure that every part of your body is completely and entirely relaxed.

Allow your mind only to wander deeper into your body now. We will proceed to relax the organs of the body by using an auto-suggestion to the internal body. Repeat in your mind after me:

Relax my physical body. My physical body is relaxing. My physical body is relaxed.

Relax my bladder. My bladder is relaxing. My bladder is relaxed.

Relax my reproductive organs. My reproductive organs are relaxing. My reproductive organs are relaxed.

Relax my small and large intestines. My intestines are relaxing. My intestines are relaxed.

Relax my stomach and pancreas. My stomach and pancreas are relaxing. My stomach and pancreas are relaxed.

Relax my spleen. My spleen is relaxing. My spleen is relaxed.

Relax my liver and my gallbladder. My liver and gallbladder are relaxing. My liver and gallbladder are relaxed.

Relax my kidneys and my adrenal glands. My kidneys and adrenal glands are relaxing. My kidneys and adrenal glands are relaxed.

Relax my lungs. My lungs are relaxing. My lungs are relaxed.

Relax my heart. My heart is relaxing. My heart is relaxed.

Relax my brain. My brain is relaxing. My brain is relaxed.

Relax all the organs in my body. All my organs are relaxing. All my organs are relaxed.

Relax my mind. I am slowing down my thoughts. I am calming down my feelings. My mind is deeply and completely relaxed.

Relax my internal body. My internal body is relaxing. My internal body is relaxed.

Take a deep breath in and out and check that your body is fully relaxed. Go deep into your subconsciousness now and allow yourself to stir with the memories and feelings that pair with the journaling that you have done for processing through your body memories. The action of processing allows all the old memories to percolate. Let them stir and come to life, and reflect and experience again, but not from the space of being a child, or whatever ages you were during these most treacherous times of your life. You are simply watching the stories as they come up and unfold. There is no remove and replace here. Nor is there a remove and release yet. The process of this work is to allow all of the memories to remove themselves from the deeply embedded tissues, bringing the stories to the front of your mind. The memories have not yet left your body. Sit with the memories. Let them show themselves to you without adding any judgments or emotions at this time. Be the observer and do not stop anything from presenting itself to you.

The processing part of this journey often can prove to be the most difficult action of all the work because it's not real-time action. It is internal action. Processing happens when you allow it to come forward and share with you all the truths that you have made excuses for not facing. In this moment, you become fully naked to the emotions and experiences of your life. Ask your body now to show you only one movie at a time. Practice this meditation with only one experience, or if it was something recurring with the same person, place, or situations, ask your body to only take you through the entire line of memories that involve those specifics. Come back and repeat this meditation with every single memory that your body wants you to experience and help it release, but be mindful not to release anything at this time. You must be able to sit in the darkness, fully exposed, and simply allow all the discomforts to rise. You might feel your body sweating or burning as you experience these one last time without trying to fight anything down.

Remove your current consciousness from your body and simply feel all the experiences that your body is asking you to witness. Stay in this space now as everything intensifies. Be strong, be fearless, be mindful, be present. Feel all of it but do not allow it to overwhelm you. Take the time now in silence to experience this single story and life event in the movie of your mind. Your body is asking for both your support and your assistance. Stay present to all.

Do not run away. Do not block anything out. Keep your mind's eye wide open and take it all in.

When you are ready to come back to the present, gently begin to wiggle your fingers and toes while keeping your eyes closed until the very end. Externalize your awareness and feel the air against your skin as you bring your thoughts into the present space. Feel the air becoming cooler around you. Take an extra-deep cleansing breath in and out and affirm to your body that you are going to listen to it and work with it, and that you deserve to heal fully from this space forward. When you are ready, open your eyes slowly and return, return, return.

Note to the Reader

The processing part of healing can be grueling and can make you feel many things, including exhaustion. Please be mindful of this aspect of the practice and care for yourself accordingly. Be gentle with yourself. Take hot baths (preferably with Epsom salts and/or sea salt). Drink extra water. Write in this journal and possibly in a separate journal more than what this book has asked you to answer. Do not share the journal with anyone as you go through. Processing is extremely personal and does not need any other voice to add to what you are doing with your own body messaging. It is not the time to seek advice or opinions from anyone who likes to offer judgment, and this includes yourself. Keep your self-talk clean and clear. Be supportive of yourself and the steps you are taking for your healing. The hardest part of it all is to be able to bring up all the memories and let them stir without action. This is the process, and it can be gnarly. This is where we cross the bridge into the good stuff, but you can't get across without this work. Therefore, be present, be vigilant, and do not move on without several repetitions of the work of this particular chapter. If it does make a lot of things feel haywire in your system, please do not hesitate to contact a professional and have them work with you as memories arise.

Chapter 7

Release

We are finally at the release portion of the action bridge! Are you ready to take a really big, deep cleansing breath with your whole entire life? Now that we have listened to our body, pulled out all the heavy carrots, filled the holes with goodness, and begun the process of rearranging how our body works, we are so close to all the fabulous emotions our body can experience! But not without the work of the release. This is the action of casting away all the attachments that have plagued us throughout our lives. It's not always just an internal healing that must take place. In many cases, it's healing ourselves by cutting out the villains in our stories. Very few of our lives' stories as told by our mental narratives or by our bodies include ourselves, right? These actions need to be taken in order to cut the cords that we have unknowingly created between ourselves and our perpetrators. In the first four chapters on all the heavy emotions, I specifically designed the meditations to be about your body and your story, without any thought about or actions toward the outside actors in our lives' movies. Now we flip that script and make it all about the outside forces that have brought us all the heavy emotions from the past to the present.

Because of the work that we did during the processing section of this book, bringing into view the whole vision of each carrot's story and everything that it entails, we are now able to put into action the part where our supporting characters and villains get killed off (semi-peacefully, of course). Let's discuss the concept of the energy cords between people and situations and how they got there. We are going to change our guided imagery now from carrots to invisible cords that connect us to other people and circumstances.

Have you ever broken up with someone and walked away heartbroken, and it seemed like they moved on without even thinking twice about you? Then sometime later, you meet someone who makes you want to forget the past, and boom! Out of what seems like nowhere, that person from the breakup calls you again. They felt the cord getting cut! When we engage with people intimately, violently, or in any significant way in between, we create a cord between ourselves and them. We may not realize that we have created this cord, and we certainly don't realize that this cord is still with us. Unless we consciously make the move to cut that cord, it will remain in place. It might lose its strong hold, but it is not gone unless we consciously choose to cut all the cords that bind us. They do not release on their own. Sometimes we cut cords unknowingly through strong intention to release ourselves from a hold that someone had over us. It can be done even if you are unaware of energy cords.

When I talk about cords, you can imagine them however feels most comfortable to you. For example, you can imagine a string or an attachment to people or places that make you feel like a dog on a chain. You want to get away, and you want to experience freedom from any pain and suffering that their presence in your life may have caused, but you may not know how to make the final break. This is it.

You must detach yourself both physically *and* energetically so they no longer have that hold on you. This is where great freedom can be found. Understand that when we truly make the commitment to engage in this level of deep work, it is in order to make a permanent change. Before you enter these practices, sit with it and determine that you are ready and willing to let go, and for the other person to let go of you. This energy runs both ways, but you have the power to cut it so that the opposite side of the cord becomes a dead end.

Without realizing it, many times we have an issue with being forgotten. Even by people who have caused us tremendous pain, we do not want to be forgotten. We want them to feel the pain that we have felt because of them. We can get stuck trying to ensure that someone feels our presence and our pain. Vendettas are a danger to ourselves. As we begin this process of cutting cords, we need to be looking at this from both perspectives. This does not only apply to the people who traumatized us. We need to take a good, long look inside and answer the question of whether we are the ones causing pain and strife to someone else. Let's admit that we have also played the role of the bad guy in someone else's story. If that is the case, you can also do the cord-cutting to free yourself by finally giving them their freedom and walking away. And for the record, we can never make someone feel the pain that we felt. If someone caused you pain, walk away without any retaliation. I talked earlier about every action having a consequence. Trust that they will get theirs, but it likely will not end up being from you. Cut the ties that bind you and allow yourself and anyone else who is attached to these cords their space to experience their life without you in it. The greatest power you have is over yourself. The strongest action that you can take when it comes to being in an unhealthy or dangerous place is to remove yourself from the equation. You are a very special and powerful human being. You deserve happiness, wholeness, and a long and healthy life. In this decision to remove cords, you are choosing yourself over all the other things. That is exactly where you want to be for this. You are worth it. It's time to step up and be brave and bold with your healing and your life. Drop those attachments and create something wonderful for yourself. That begins here. Your liberation is the destination.

In Preparation for Cord-Cutting

Before we begin, there are several details I want to lay out for you so that you can be well prepared for this meditation exercise. A cord-cutting can be done with multiple lines at one time, or one single line directly to one person or situation. It can be like collecting several lines, just as we would pull a section of hair up and line it up in order to cut it straight across and halfway down. Cutting several lines at one time would include memories that have more than just a couple of people. These old memories could be from wartime, from a classroom, from a school, from a hospital, and so on. Collect all the energy lines (which will be thinner but still attached nonetheless) and envision them like gathering strands of hair or thin wires. When it is one-on-one, the cord is more like a thick, tight rope, like the kind you used to climb in PE class, connected from your point of entry to theirs. If it is something or someone you once loved, the cords likely connect from your heart space to theirs. If it was something traumatic and abusive, the cords likely connect from the place of assault fired from one side and landing in another. This could be a cord between one person's hands and the other person's receiving point. It is also important to understand that the cords run both directions; it is never one-sided. Even an attacker will not be able to walk away and never think about what happened again. You are connected now. There has been a cord that inserted itself at the point of entry at the moment that it occurred.

Some cords also need to be cut, not because you want them to be gone from your life or memory, but because you have been operating with a heaviness that brings both parties down. For example, as I have mentioned, I lost my father when I was thirteen years old. He was my favorite person in the world, and the loss was sudden and shocking to my system. When I was in my late twenties, I was diagnosed with PTSD and sought help for the trauma that had never changed from that day on, so many years before. I went through a healing practice known as EMDR (eye movement desensitization and reprocessing) therapy to help me reprocess the trauma. I actually had a cord-cutting session between myself and my father with the heavy rope between our hearts. The therapist never led me this way; it happened all on its own organically as the image and work that I needed. No one had ever taught me about cord-cutting back then. I had never heard of it before. I believe my dad brought me to that place to finally set me on a path to stop living my life only halfway. I think many of us who have experienced deep loss feel a sense of guilt in moving forward with our lives. It seems that every time we feel joy, we feel a sense of guilt that we are present at that moment and embracing it without that loved one there with us. I had a very hard time cutting the rope because I feared it meant I was cutting him from my life. In my own meditation work with this practice, my dad actually handed me the scissors. To my surprise, once I removed the rope from my heart and from his, he was able to come to me and hold me tightly without that heavy rope that tied us. Until that moment, I never realized that the cord I kept was damaging instead of loving. It weighed us down. Just because you choose to cut a cord does not mean that you have to cut other people fully away. It means that whatever binder that kept it so heavy can be removed during this practice. It needs to be accompanied with the sincere intention of what you would like the outcome to be. I believe that my dad was finally able to come and speak to me and give me the tools I needed to live my life here and not feel so guilty about it. I offer this specific practice to you based entirely on my own life experience. It changed my life, and I hope it can help do the same for you.

Add the Eyes

We will change this meditation practice slightly to prepare ourselves for the cord-cutting. Based on research behind EMDR therapy, there is a connection between conscious eye movement and the release of fear held within the part of the amygdala that relates to fear learning.[24] While we will not be consciously moving our eyes while we are accessing the situations to cut the cords to them, we will add in a full eye movement practice as part of the relaxation phase in order to activate that area of the brain for this particular work.

Meditation Tips

We will relax into our meditation the same way that we have for every practice in this book. Then, we will veer off into the cord-cutting action rather than going deeper into any body scans. Remember to practice each cord-cutting meditation with only one scenario or person at a time. This practice should be repeated as needed for every experience that you need to release from your past in order to claim a much brighter future. Please follow up with the journal entries (do it on additional pieces of paper if you run out of space here) for best results and to confirm the work that was accomplished through this meditation.

Be sure to use the bathroom before beginning this practice. Each practice will take approximately 15 to 20 minutes to complete. Lie down in a place where you will be comfortable and not distracted. Turn down the lights, preferably having only natural light in the room. Be sure you are wearing nonrestrictive clothing. Remember to go to www.emilyafrancisbooks.com and click on the audio link to receive the meditation.

Audio and Written Meditation

Before lying down, do the eye practice while seated. Look up to the ceiling. Look down to the floor. Look straight up. Look straight down. Look to your right side and then all the way to the left. Look to your right and again to your left. We will now do full circles with our eyes. Begin with looking at the floor, to your right, up to the ceiling, to your left, and back to the floor. Once you are looking at the floor, do the same circle but in the opposite direction. Down, left, up, and right, and then return to looking back at the floor. From there, gently close your eyes and allow your eyes to relax. Now you can lie down and get comfortable, or assume whatever position you prefer for the following meditation.

Allow your legs to relax and your feet to fall out naturally to each side. Bring your arms out slightly from your body and have the palms facing up.

Allow your arms and your legs to be far enough from the center line of your body that they are able to comfortably lie straight without tension. Allow your arms and legs to hang like the limbs of a rag doll. Let your arms and legs begin to feel heavy and limp. Feel your spine straighten and become heavy on the surface beneath you. Roll your head from side to side and then settle comfortably in the middle. Exhale all of the breath from your body.

Now, take a slow, comfortable, full breath in through the nose, and exhale completely through the mouth. Make the sound *ahhhh* on just the first deep release to signal to the nervous system that it is time to relax. Breathe in: 1 . . . 2 . . . 3 . . . 4 . . . Hold the breath without tension in the body. Exhale for 1 . . . 2 . . . 3 . . . 4 . . . 5 . . . 6 . . . 7 . . . 8 . . . Hold that space without the breath before inhaling again. Slow your breathing and allow the breath to set the tone for your relaxation.

Focus on your feet and tighten them by pointing and flexing your feet up and down slowly to the rhythm of your breath. Relax your feet. Relax your shins and calf muscles. Allow your knees to soften. Feel the tops of your thighs and the back sides of your legs relax. Inhale and hold your breath now. Tighten every single part of the legs and feet and lift your feet one inch off the surface beneath you. Exhale and allow your legs and feet to drop. Slowly inhale and clench your buttocks, then lift your buttocks and hips off the surface beneath you. Hold your breath as you lift up and tighten the muscles. Exhale and slowly lower down, and tuck the hips under, allowing your lower back to lie flat on the surface beneath you. Inhale and hold your breath, arch your back, and lift your entire middle and upper back off the surface beneath you. Exhale and slowly lower down. Inhale and lift your shoulders up toward your ears. Hold your breath as your shoulders are raised as high as they can go. Exhale and lower the shoulders down. Inhale and hold your breath. Tighten your arms and make a fist with your hands. Lift your arms and hands one inch off the surface beneath you. Exhale and feel the heat and heaviness unwind from the tops of your shoulders, down the upper arms, around the elbows, the forearms and wrists, into the palms of your hands, and off each fingertip as you lower your arms down and relax your hands. Inhale and hold your breath. Squeeze your face, tighten your eyelids, and clench your jaw. Exhale and relax your face. Inhale and hold your breath for a moment. Exhale and open your mouth, stick your tongue out as far as you can, open your eyes wide, and try to bring your eyebrows up to the top of your hairline. As you stick your tongue out and exhale, make the *ahhh* sound again, signaling your body to let go. Once you have released the final audible exhalation, gently relax your entire face. Relax your ears. Relax your scalp and every hair on your head. Breathe slowly and deeply without pressure. Gently bring your awareness all the way up and down your entire physical body, making sure that every part of your body is completely and entirely relaxed.

Allow your mind to wander deeper into your body now. We will proceed to relax the organs of the body by using an auto-suggestion. Repeat in your mind after me:

I am relaxing my body. My body is relaxing. My body is relaxed.

I am relaxing my bladder. My bladder is relaxing. My bladder is relaxed.

I am relaxing the reproductive organs of my body. My reproductive organs are relaxing. My reproductive organs are relaxed.

I am relaxing my small and large intestines. My intestines are relaxing. My intestines are relaxed.

I am relaxing my stomach and pancreas. My stomach and pancreas are relaxing. My stomach and pancreas are relaxed.

I am relaxing my spleen. My spleen is relaxing. My spleen is relaxed.

I am relaxing my liver and my gallbladder. My liver and gallbladder are relaxing. My liver and gallbladder are relaxed.

I am relaxing my kidneys and my adrenal glands. My kidneys and adrenal glands are relaxing. My kidneys and adrenal glands are relaxed.

I am relaxing my lungs. My lungs are relaxing. My lungs are relaxed.

I am relaxing my heart. My heart is relaxing. My heart is relaxed.

I am relaxing my brain. My brain is relaxing. My brain is relaxed.

I am relaxing all the organs in my body. All my organs are relaxing. All my organs are relaxed.

I am relaxing my mind. I am slowing down my thoughts. I am calming down my feelings. My mind is deeply and completely relaxed.

I am relaxing my entire body. My whole body is relaxing. My whole body is relaxed.

Once your entire body is fully relaxed, bring your awareness to only one person or situation that requires releasing. Take a deep breath and fully decide in this moment that you are prepared to allow the heavy connection to be cut from your life. This does not mean that the experiences or memories are erased, but it will offer the opportunity for the dialogue and the energy that surround the connection to diminish significantly. Take a moment and affirm to yourself that you are in full agreement with your mind and body to cut the cord that connects you to this person or event. Continue to breathe slowly and fully, and keep your mind completely focused on the task ahead. Bring the person or situation into full vision in your mind's eye. See the situation as it happened without any added narration. Allow yourself to semi-experience the situation once more, but from the point of the observer. You are not experiencing this in your body again. You are simply watching them. You are watching you. You are gathering up all the memories that surround this person or experience. Hold the memory steady in the middle of your conscious vision. Decide what method you would like to use to cut the cords between you. Does the situation involve more than one person besides yourself? If so, gather all the cords at once, lift them up, and put them together. If it is one person, see the thick rope from you to them and notice where the points of entry are for both of you. Keep your vision strong and stay focused throughout this practice. Do not let your mind wander or question. Be strong in your conviction as you face the final release action. In your mental picture, you can be seated or standing across from this person. Whichever you choose, get comfortable and steady as you now choose what size scissors to use to cut through the rope.

In your mind, reach with your dominant hand, pick up the sharpest and largest scissors you can envision, and open them below the cord in the middle between you and them. Inhale and hold your breath for a moment. Exhale, and cut all the way through the cord. Feel every fiber of the rope beginning to tear apart and fall down. Each point of entry still holding the cord remains in place in your body and theirs, but the cord is no longer connected. See the two ends of the cord fall to the ground between you. Pull the cord that is dangling from your body all the way out of you. As you pull slowly and deliberately, feel the cord pulling through you and then fully out of your body. Drop that cord on the ground. The space that is opened from that rope evaporates as quickly as it opens. Cord-cutting can offer self-healing instantly if you choose for it to be so. Close the space within yourself quickly. Affirm that you are healed and there is no scar tissue from removing this cord. If for any reason it does not feel that way to you, use the same buckets with the colors that we used in our previous work to fill the space left open. Trust your own choice here and know that it is safe, healthy, and covered.

It is entirely up to you if you choose to pull the cord out from the other side as well or leave it and only focus on yourself for this. If you do pull their rope, do so quickly, with intention and no eye contact or discussion. If you are unable to do that as you approach them, then do not include them in this work. If you are so kind, you can pull from their side for them and drop it on the ground. If it was something violent, leave it without guilt or attachment. This cord is not about them whatsoever. It is about you—your body, the effects of those cords, the new effects without the cords, and your overall health and well-being. Do not walk away quickly from the work you've just done. Sit with it. Breathe into it. Be open in your mind to what just occurred.

Affirm that you are now able to move forward with your life without carrying the burdens that these bonds have placed on you. Your body is now able to regenerate and function at levels you have not experienced before. Breathe with a new confidence and lightness. Look inside yourself and see if you can notice the cells in your body beginning to function more peacefully. Notice your cells begin to reprogram themselves to function at optimum levels now. If the ends of the rope were bloody, let them remain bloody. No cleanup is needed in this space. Leave them all on the floor. Take another solid cleansing breath and decide to walk away from this with the confidence that you are now facing a new direction toward your very best life.

When you are ready, begin to bring yourself back into your body. Wiggle your fingers and your toes. Feel the air on your skin. Externalize your awareness. Feel the air against your nostrils as your breath returns to normal. Take all the time you need before turning on one side and helping yourself to sit back up. When you are ready, return, return, return.

Congratulate yourself for a job well done. It takes strength and courage to finally release the ties that bind and the heaviness we have grown so accustomed to carrying. You are free. Believe it. Trust it. Embrace it. You earned it. Repeat this meditation for every person, situation, or event that you need to release.

Repeat this affirmation: ***Every cell in my body is reprogramming itself to function at healthy, optimum levels now.***

Journal

Who or what was this cord connected to?

Where was the cord connected in your body?

What was the cord connected to? Was it connected to another person's body, or was it connected to a place or situation, and where were those cords on the other side?

How do you feel following the release of the cord?

Do you trust yourself to let these cords die there?

Please do not try to run back or recreate damaging things in your life simply because you don't yet know how to function without them. Be very mindful with this practice. It is real. You must have affirmative thoughts to back up the work you just completed. Trust that this really happened and the work you did inside yourself will carry through into the physical. This is a true cord-connection release. You have finally cut it out and away from you. This might leave you feeling naked, raw, vulnerable, and exposed. We don't know how to live without those pains and shames that have lived inside us for so long. Be patient with yourself as you allow yourself the experience to feel whole and healthy. You are giving yourself the freedom to heal. *Take it and try not to look back.*

Create an affirmation based on the cord that has been cut and what you intend to do with the new lightness.

Pairing the Affirmation with a Hand Position or Mudra

When we create an affirmation to repeat following our deep meditation work, it is important that we also pair the practice with a specific touch on the body to fully activate and align both the tissue memory patterns along with the mental groove sets. There are many options to dialogue deeply with the body. Feel free to explore all of these suggestions and choose which of these work best for you and your specific work. My top suggestions are:

The two-hand touch involves placing your left middle fingertip directly over the navel. The left hand is the receiving hand. In Chinese medicine this is the CV8 point. The CV8 translates to the "spirit gate." This is a point of integration to help recalibrate your current energy to match "the vibrational remedy that is placed upon it."[12]

Place the right middle fingertip on the top of the head at the midline. The right hand is considered the giving hand. This point in Chinese medicine is known as the *baijiu* or the DU20 point. This point translates to "the meeting of the hundreds." It is the place where all energies within the body converge and meet.[13]

The specific point to be aware of is the spot where we first touch the tips of the ears and meet our fingers together at the top of the head. In or around that area will be an incredibly slight dip in that suture line. That is the spot to touch. Once you find it, you'll be able to locate it with ease moving forward.

An affirmation you can say while holding the hands in the two positions is: "I allow my body to heal deeply and completely." A more detailed affirmation might be needed according to the work that you have just completed. The affirmation you choose is entirely up to you.

Prayer hands is the most notable hand position or mudra known worldwide to prepare and activate our connection to the heavens as well as to activate the clearing of the mind and the opening of the heart space. Prayer hands asks that God enter our work and help us to clear and heal.

Mudras include touching together specific fingers to activate a certain energy and intention. The most basic hand mudra besides prayer hands is to connect the first finger to the thumb (chin mudra) to connect yourself with the universe. The index finger represents you, and the thumb represents the universe. How you naturally place the two fingers together can give insight into where you are in relation with the universe. Tucking the finger under the thumb indicates that you are bowing down to the universe. Meeting tip to tip would indicate that you feel even with the universe: not above or beneath the energy itself.

Section III

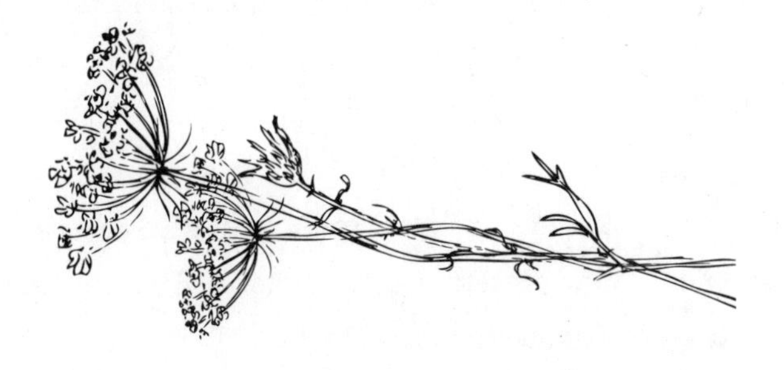

The Fabulous Four

The fabulous four are the light side of body experiences, but no less powerful. In fact, these body emotions carry us to improved health and vitality. These four emotions are specific in their nature, yet you will find that they overlap and work together to create the final emotion, which is a true sense of empowerment. Happiness is an emotion that is experienced in the present moment. Adding happy experiences and repeating those feelings create tracks through the memory systems that we retrieve to be reminded of how it feels to be functioning at our happiest and healthiest levels. It is impossible to experience bliss and fear at the same time. They cannot coexist. There is not room for both at the same time, and in each moment of the present, we must choose. Learning to scan the body and use the good stuff to set us back on the healthy track are where the real power lies. The fabulous four go in order of intensity from being happy, to joy, leading into becoming connected, and finally when all of those are in place and fully realized, we become empowered.

What I learned through writing this book that I find so exciting is that wild carrots can grow beautiful flowers from their stems called Queen Anne's lace (which is the art at the beginning of this section). I've seen Queen Anne's lace my whole life along the highway and would always get excited when I saw the plants, but I never thought there might be a carrot under the surface! God always has a plan and leaves us secret treasures to discover along the way, both along the road and within ourselves. In these next chapters, we will discover the lighter side of the body's emotions. We will still be looking for carrots in our meditations, but this time we will not be *removing* and *replacing* or *removing* and *releasing*, but instead we will add the new practice of *picking* and *planting*. We will gently pinch off a flower bud from each carrot and plant it someplace else in our body to grow more of that goodness within.

Chapter 8
Happy

There is a whole other side to body emotions that often gets overlooked. Just as the soft tissues store memories of trauma, they also store the lighter and more loving ones. We are actually hardwired for pursuing happiness as humans. In fact, scientific research has proven that positive emotions actually enhance the association memories of emotions from positive experiences.[25] Science now shows that emotions in the brain, both positive and negative, are stored within the amygdala but not in the same location within the amygdala itself. Research on mice at the RIKEN-MIT Center for Neural Circuit Genetics demonstrated that positive neurons are found in the back of the amygdala and negative neuron activity was found in the front of the amygdala.[26] The amygdala is what attaches the emotions to the memories themselves. Using positive memories to help heal our bodies is an untapped treasure that we have not learned enough about. Just as our stories can revolve around our life's traumas, so, too, can they revolve around the positive events in our life when we simply allow ourselves to experience pleasure and feel happy, elated, or blissful. Those are present-moment emotions, and they are just as valuable to our bodies as they are in the mind. Real happiness, the kind that comes with the small things that others might dismiss or the big things that tickle your soul, is the experience that expands within the tissues. We feel happy when we hear a song come on that brings back really fond memories. The whole body lights up in remembrance. Or when we do an exercise that we used to love to do and haven't done in a while, our bodies tend to rejoice in the movements, not just because we are engaging in something healthy, but because we are engaging in something memorably joyful. Smelling something delightful can bring back intense sensations within our memory systems. Smell is the strongest of all the senses when memory is concerned.[26]

Happiness is an emotion that is experienced in the present moment. It can also be related to a general sense of well-being.[27] It is the first of my four fabulous emotions because everyone can relate to the experience of feeling happy. Feeling happy can be fleeting as an experience, but the body understands and easily remembers each and every time that the particular happy hormones release. The hormones that are released when we experience happiness are dopamine, serotonin, oxytocin, and endorphins.[28] As a brief overview, the breakdown of chemicals for happiness is important. For example, oxytocin is responsible for our social abilities. Serotonin gives us the strength to push through and stay positive. Serotonin governs our moods. A good mood comes from serotonin, while a bad mood comes from lack of it. Endorphins rush through when we are facing a fight, flight, or freeze situation. Endorphins release whether we feel terrified or excited. It's physiologically a very similar experience. Do you remember the movie *Legally Blonde*? Elle Woods makes a statement about endorphins. She said quite wisely, "Exercise gives you endorphins. Endorphins make you happy. Happy people just don't shoot their husbands; they just don't!"[29] When it comes to dopamine, we hear a good bit about the dopamine receptors and we believe that they release when we feel giddy and happy, but they actually release just before we experience the feelings. Dopamine releases at the anticipation of happy feelings. This means that in visualization practices of experiences, we can still release dopamine, even if we are not in the actual fields of gold dancing around the flowers. In our meditations in these four chapters, it is possible to release the hormones through our practice and learn to do more of the same.

Let's talk muscles of facial expression. When we are happy, we smile, open our mouths and laugh, and maybe cry happy tears. All of this requires specific muscle activation based on our emotions. Smiling engages muscles that relay to the brain and signal the release of hormones that improve health and vitality. It takes more muscles to smile than it does to frown. The smile muscles are used much more often than the frown muscles and therefore are generally stronger and have a deeper memory track into the muscles that govern them.[30] Naturally, when we are in the moment of feeling happy, we smile a real smile. How much do we adore the moments when our face hurts from laughing too much? That is the experience of happiness! It's in real time, fully in the present. There is even research that indicates that when we activate the smile muscles, we tend to find things more humorous. Researchers found this by placing a pencil horizontally between the top and bottom molars. This put the muscles into the smile response. The muscles were engaged, and there was a release of the happiness hormones. It's a chain reaction of all the best things. Conversely, they did the same study but placed the pencil facing front to back, and had the subjects bite down with the front teeth and activate the scowl muscles by holding the lips tightly around the pencil. The body had a different response. It found the same stimulus less humorous.[31] This is just by simply activating the muscles of facial expressions: the smiles and the scowl!

The wonderful thing about happy experiences is that we can build more happiness at any time, and I want you to! Think about when a baby smiles; it's real. Their eyes light up, their belly moves when they laugh, and their whole face glows. When was the last time you felt happy like that? I hope your answer is very recently. Happy is the lightest of the fabulous four because of how present in time it is. It embeds into the body, but not as deeply as the other fabulous emotions. This is the experience that needs more of itself in order to go deeper into your memory tracks. Therefore, I encourage you to search daily for something that makes you laugh really hard.

I also ask that you give yourself permission and the time to be completely present in the moment when you feel happiness wash over you. Close your eyes, savor the moment, and try to keep it to use again later. Take a mental photo of the things that make you feel fully alive, and bring them to the front of your memory as often as you can. Like attracts like. The more you allow happy feelings inside, the more you will have them. When you experience high vibrations of happiness, you can experience sheer bliss. And the great thing about experiencing the emotion of feeling blissfully happy? It never runs out of itself! It's a never-ending well, multiplying itself all the time. If you don't know where to start, go with something easy; put on a hilarious movie that you love and let yourself experience deep belly laughs without restriction. Or put on a comedy show that you love. Or go visit your local improv comedy theater if you have one.

Those will delight your whole body. Once you get into the habit of allowing yourself to laugh and feel happy, you will find happiness in more places than you ever knew were possible. Maybe consider taking a laughter yoga class. Do whatever you can to experience happiness, laughter, good vibrations, and bliss. Laughter yoga has much science and research behind it on the incredible benefits to your health.[14]

The meditations in this section are very similar to those in the other sections, but now focus on the light side of the body experiences for a reason. I chose to keep the meditations and journal writings uniform because the results are embedded deeper into your consciousness that way. It becomes a user-friendly tool that is available for you to practice on your own without this guidance. As you enter these meditations and are shown memories that planted into your body from feeling happy, do not be afraid to have a smile on your face at any time throughout the practice. The smile opens you up to greater awareness and a deeper track into your memory systems.

Meditation Tips

You will find that for the fabulous four emotions, the meditation and the journaling are again similar to those for the heavy four. This is for consistency in allowing the body to learn new patterns of acceptance. Please approach each meditation practice as if it is new, even when you begin to familiarize yourself with the pattern.

Be sure to use the bathroom before beginning this practice. Each practice will take approximately 15 to 20 minutes to complete. Lie down in a place where you will be comfortable and without distractions. Turn down the lights, preferably having only natural light in the room. Lie down either on the floor, a couch, or a bed. If you prefer to be seated, this works as well. Be sure you are wearing nonrestrictive clothing.

We will relax every part of the external body. Then we will relax deeper into the organs through auto-suggestion and then begin the process of doing the body scan and working with each individual budding flower from the carrot. Keep in mind that we only work with a single carrot bloom per meditation practice. I encourage you to return to the same meditation over and over until you feel the effects from every flower bloom that was planted. Continue with this practice until you feel that every available emotion has multiplied as much as it possibly can before you move on to the next set of positive emotions. You can fill out the journal and mark on the body as you repeat each practice.

Once you are finished with the meditation, you will document where you found this particular carrot bloom in your body. You will also document the location of the carrot as well as where you planted the new bloom. I also ask that you record the name that you gave each carrot bloom so that you are able to recall what memory went with what practice. Remember to go to www.emilyafrancisbooks.com and click on the audio link to receive the meditation.

Audio and Written Meditation

Allow your legs to relax and your feet to fall out naturally to each side. Bring your arms out slightly from your body and have the palms facing up. Allow your arms and your legs to be far enough from the center line of your body that they can comfortably lie straight without tension. Allow your arms and legs to hang like the limbs of a rag doll. Let your arms and legs begin to feel heavy and limp. Feel your spine straighten and become heavy on the surface beneath you. Roll your head from side to side, and then settle comfortably in the middle. Exhale all the breath from your body. Now take a slow, comfortable, full breath in through the nose, and exhale completely through the mouth. Make the sound *ahhh* on just the first deep release to signal to the nervous system that it is time for it to relax. Breathe in, 1 . . . 2 . . . 3 . . . 4 . . . Hold the breath without tension in your body. Exhale, 1 . . . 2 . . . 3 . . . 4 . . . 5 . . . 6 . . . 7 . . . 8 . . . Hold that space without the breath before inhaling again. Slow your breathing and allow the breath to set the tone for your relaxation.

Begin with your feet and tighten them by pointing and flexing them up and down slowly to the rhythm of your breath. Then relax your feet. Relax your shins and calf muscles. Allow your knees to soften. Feel the tops of your thighs and the back sides of the legs relax. Inhale and hold your breath now. Tighten every part of your legs and feet, and lift your feet one inch off the surface beneath you. Exhale and allow your legs and feet to drop. Slowly inhale and clench your buttocks and lift the buttocks and hips off the surface beneath you. Hold your breath as you lift up and tighten the muscles. Exhale and slowly lower down and tuck the hips under you, allowing your lower back to lie flat on the surface beneath you. Inhale and hold your breath, arch your back, and lift your entire middle and upper back off the surface beneath you. Exhale and slowly lower down. Inhale and lift your shoulders up toward your ears. Hold your breath as your shoulders are raised as high as they can go. Exhale and lower your shoulders down. Inhale and hold the breath. Tighten the arms and make a fist with your hands. Lift your arms and hands one inch off the surface beneath you. Exhale and feel the heat and heaviness unwind from the tops of your shoulders, down the upper arms, around the elbows, the forearms and wrists, into the palms of your hands, and off each fingertip as you lower your arms down and relax your hands. Inhale and hold your breath. Squeeze your face, tighten your eyelids, and clench your jaw. Exhale and relax your face. Inhale and hold your breath for a moment. Exhale and open your mouth, stick your tongue out as far as you can, open your eyes wide, and try to bring your eyebrows up to the top of your hairline. As you stick your tongue out and exhale, make the *ahhh* sound again, signaling to your central nervous system to relax and let go. Once you have released the final audible exhalation, gently relax your entire face. Relax your ears. Relax your scalp and every hair on your head. Breathe slowly and deeply without pressure. Gently bring your awareness all the way up and down your entire physical body, making sure that every part of your body is completely and entirely relaxed.

Allow your mind to wander deeper into your body now. We will proceed to relax the organs of the body by using an auto-suggestion. Repeat in your mind after me:

I am relaxing my entire body. My body is relaxing. My body is relaxed.

I am relaxing my bladder. My bladder is relaxing. My bladder is relaxed.

I am relaxing the reproductive organs of my body. My reproductive organs are relaxing. My reproductive organs are relaxed.

I am relaxing my small and large intestines. My intestines are relaxing. My intestines are relaxed.

I am relaxing my stomach and pancreas. My stomach and pancreas are relaxing. My stomach and pancreas are relaxed.

I am relaxing my spleen. My spleen is relaxing. My spleen is relaxed.

I am relaxing my liver and my gallbladder. My liver and gallbladder are relaxing. My liver and gallbladder are relaxed.

I am relaxing my kidneys and my adrenal glands. My kidneys and adrenal glands are relaxing. My kidneys and adrenal glands are relaxed.

I am relaxing my lungs. My lungs are relaxing. My lungs are relaxed.

I am relaxing my heart. My heart is relaxing. My heart is relaxed.

I am relaxing my brain. My brain is relaxing. My brain is relaxed.

I am relaxing all the organs in my body. All my organs are relaxing. All my organs are relaxed.

Relax my mind. I am slowing down my thoughts. I am calming down my feelings. My mind is deeply and completely relaxed.

I am relaxing my entire body. My entire body is relaxing. My entire body is relaxed.

Now bring your awareness into the deepest, darkest, most hidden parts of your body. Go into the bloodstream now and gently surf through your body inside the blood and plasma. Use this liquid flow to guide you throughout your entire body one full time. Become an observer of the way your body flows beneath the surface. Bring yourself into the darkness where the master factory of the muscles, fasciae, and other soft tissues are at work keeping you alive and healthy. Once you have scanned and surfed through your own flow of movement within, allow your eyes to turn inward and go anywhere that your body asks you to go. We begin to scan the entire body all the way from the top of the head to the bottoms of the feet. Now go deeper into the layer that is almost never seen, into your sacred garden. All we can see is deep, dark soil laid out through every channel of your body. This is the deepest layer of our being where only the garden lives. Within the soil are rows of carrots. We are now scanning the garden for carrots that not only have green tops, but also have flower blossoms growing beyond the green bunch of the carrot. The flower blooms are usually white in color but can have light hues of various pastel colors. These flowers have bloomed from the carrots that are implanted in your body because of emotions that were happy and loving experiences.

Look closely as you begin to notice very small blossoms of soft-colored flowers growing just above the surface. Discover your garden however you like, whether by walking slowly up and down the lines of the soil, scanning with your eyes, using your sense of smell for something light and fragrant, or gently moving your hands across the body soil in search of soft flower buds growing from the tops of the carrots. It is your practice and your choice on how to connect deeply into the spaces where you have planted a harvest. We set our intentions in this deep space that our body opens up to us and unites with our consciousness for our greatest good and strongest health now. The messages of the body are subtle, and you must be open to receive them. In this space, we are able to gently pull a few of the blooms and replant them in other areas of the body in order to increase the positive emotions throughout.

Think of the word ***happy***. We now open ourselves up to any messages, images, or flashes of light or color that catch our eye to what comes with the thought of *happy*. Notice when that word enters your consciousness that one flash of color will light up from somewhere deep inside your inner garden. Look for the soft blooms of lighter and more loving experiences of being *happy* during various times of your life. Notice now that one of the flower blooms has alerted you to its presence. Bring all your awareness to this one carrot. In your mind's eye, imagine a tiny version of your whole self going next to this carrot and sitting down beside it. None of this should be approached quickly. Each carrot has planted itself into the area and grown deep roots from the time of its inception. Be gentle as you look, listen, and ask this carrot to tell you how it got there. Allow the carrot that represents this first round of *happy* to tell you its story. Not your story. Not the story that you have been telling yourself all this time. Allow the emotion from the *happy* times to wash over you and share images and feelings with you from that time. Bask in this moment to relive again as if it was happening in real time. Maybe people whom you have loved and lost show up in these images. Maybe it is something with just yourself. Whatever stories are shared, they are from the flower that bloomed because of the experience. Be grateful but do not get ahead of your thoughts. Let the flower tell you its story and take you back in time with it.

Once it shares with you an image or an actual story, feel free to name that flower bloom. Name it something to assure that its story is heard, you understand its meaning, and you are thankful to be reminded of it. Ask the carrot, by its new name, if it would be all right if you pulled out just a few of the blooms in order to plant them in other parts of your body for increased *happy*, health, and love. Once you feel the carrot has given you permission to pull out and plant the flowers, see yourself taking one hand and gently pinching off those blooms to replant elsewhere. These are the blooms that embraced life fully, that allowed you to truly enjoy the feeling of being *happy*. Embrace the sensations as they wash over you and remind you just how sweet and pleasant life can be. This is your life! It is yours to make new in this moment and to begin again by planting a bountiful harvest that you have sowed in your life.

Place a single word of intention into this area to grow and radiate out into your body. What do you hope for in feeling the refreshing laughter and love and health and healing from feeling so *happy*? Now place a bloom that you have gently pinched off and plant it in another part of your body that needs love and healing. Affirm that those blooms will now grow new roots and help you heal yourself from within. Gently smile and feel the power of intention in your healing. Be sure to give thanks to both the carrot with the flower and the newly planted bloom. Breathe deeply into this space and when you are ready, take your awareness back up a few layers, until you can feel the air on your skin. Breathe slowly and deeply, and keep your eyes closed until the very end. Gently begin to wiggle your fingers and your toes. Notice the air becoming cooler with each breath. Feel the air on your skin and bring your awareness back into the room you are lying in, and now fully into your external body. When you are ready, and with a renewed sense of purpose and light, open your eyes and return, return, return.

Journal

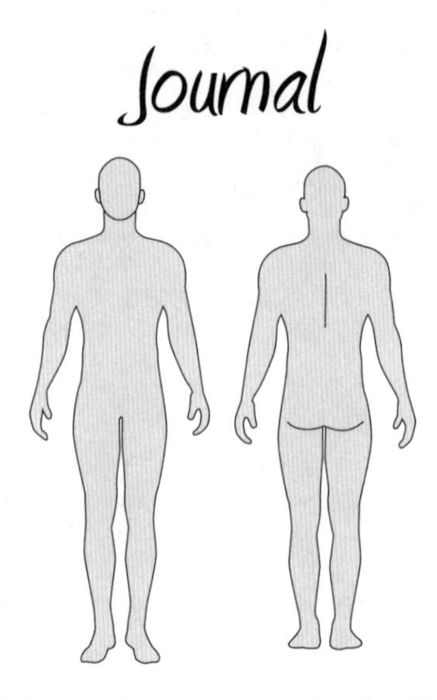

Happy What wild carrot bloom presented itself to you when you meditated on the concept of feeling happy?

Where was that carrot bloom located in your body?

___

How did it show itself to you?

___

What was the story that the carrot shared with you?

___

How did it make you feel when you experienced it again?

___

How was it different from the story that you identify with in that particular circumstance?

___

___

Did you learn anything from what the carrot had to share with you?

____

What did the flowers look like? What color were they?

____

What name did you give to the bloom for this story?

____

Where did you plant the new bloom in your body, and why did you choose that place?

____

____

How do you feel in your body now after planting flowers in other areas of the body?

____

____

Allowing the happy emotions to enter your body means being courageous and trusting that you are allowed to be happy. You are allowed to heal. Believe it or not, accepting healing and that we deserve to heal requires follow-up measures to continue to confirm this new decision. I suggest you choose from the following: counseling, writing yourself a letter, placing your hand over that place in your body coupled with an affirmation allowing that new healing to remain, or writing how you feel and putting it on your mirror or someplace where you can see it daily. Make a commitment now to follow through with this work to make sure that the new blooms are growing and multiplying in your body. You must be willing to give yourself permission to experience happiness in your life and inside your body. Give yourself full permission in this space to trust that the new blooms you planted will help your body to mend, recover, renew, nourish, and have faith in the path ahead. You deserve all the happiness, light, love, and radiant health.

Repeat the following affirmation: *I deserve all the happiness, light, love, and radiant health that are coming to me now. I am happy. I am healthy. I am strong. I am healing.*

Pairing the Affirmation with a Hand Position or Mudra

When we create an affirmation to repeat following our deep meditation work, it is important that we also pair the practice with a specific touch to the body to fully activate and align both the tissue memory patterns along with the mental groove sets. There are many options to dialogue deeply with the body. Feel free to explore all these suggestions and choose which of these work best for you and your specific work.

The two-hand touch involves placing the tip of your left middle finger directly on your navel. The left hand is the receiving hand. In Chinese medicine this is the CV8 point. The CV8 translates to the "spirit gate." This is a point of integration to help recalibrate your current energy to match "the vibrational remedy that is placed upon it."[12] Place the right middle fingertip directly on the top of the head at the midline. The right hand is considered the giving hand. This point in Chinese medicine is known as the *baijiu* or the DU20 point. This point translates to "the meeting of the hundreds." It is the place where all the energies within the body "converge and meet."[13]

The specific point to be aware of is the spot where we first touch the tips of the ears and let our fingers meet together at the top of the head. In or around that area will be an incredibly slight dip in that suture line. That is the spot to touch. Once you find it, you'll be able to locate it with ease moving forward.

Prayer hands is the most notable hand position or mudra known worldwide to prepare and activate our connection to the heavens as well as to activate the clearing of the mind and the opening of the heart space. Prayer hands asks that God enter our work and help us to clear and heal.

Mudras include touching together specific fingers to activate a certain energy and intention. The most basic hand mudra besides prayer hands is to connect the first finger to the thumb (chin mudra) to connect yourself with the universe. The index finger represents you, and the thumb represents the universe. How you naturally place the two fingers together can give insight into where you are in relation with the universe. Tucking the finger under the thumb indicates that you are bowing down to the universe. Meeting tip to tip would indicate that you feel even with the universe: not above or beneath the energy itself.

Chapter 9

Joy

When researching the difference between happiness and joy, Rachel Fearnley found that, "joy and happiness are wonderful feelings to experience, but are very different. Joy is more consistent and cultivated internally. It comes when you make peace with who you are, why you are and how you are, whereas happiness tends to be externally triggered."[32] When I think of joy within the body, it is a physiology that you can actually track within the system. As I said previously, feelings of happiness tend to be in the present time, whereas joy goes deeper into the muscle memory and other memory tracks. Joy is the best emotion to work with and pull up from the body in order to produce more of the same. The body recognizes the experience. Joy is deeply felt and experienced, and it tends to last longer than feelings of happiness. In my opinion, joy is the fountain of youth for the body. It releases all the hormones you want to be released. It activates the brain, the muscles, the tissues, and the mind in all the best ways. Joy is not a flighty experience. It is a deeply felt experience. Joy is what we need to tap into when we are faced with healing our bodies in big ways. Joy comes with a sense of peace that washes over the body internally. When you engage in practices such as mindfulness, meditation, affirmations, or visualizations, you can pull the joy from the experience to multiply itself. Though not nearly as much research has been done on the positive side of emotions as on traumatic ones, these somatic emotions are a true source of liberation from dis-ease.

As an example, many years ago my best friend and I took off and went to the beach for a weekend getaway. We didn't plan a beach vacation; we didn't reserve a hotel room. We just drove until we found a good destination. It was a perfect weekend, despite staying in a motel where an actual crime scene was going on. We spent the days by the water. We sat in innertubes at the edge of the water and were in that perfect spot where the water comes up over you but it doesn't wipe you out or cover your face. She was an improv comedian and had me rolling in stitches of laughter. When we got home, my face hurt for a week because it was so sore from laughing deeply. In remembering that time, I can still feel the whole memory as if it were yesterday, even though it was more than ten years ago. It is so deeply entrenched in my memory. My body can feel it much the same way as my mind. I can remember the salty water, the feel of the sun, the smell in the air. All my senses were fully engaged. I was completely present in the moment, and my body remembers it clearly. It is in those physiological experiences where the body is equally present that the tissues become the bedding where the memories lie. And that is how the tracks get laid. That is the experience of joy.

For some reason, we quite often tend to vacillate between feeling joy and feeling guilt for embracing the joy. That is a teeter-totter behavior pattern that I want you to become mindful of, and I ask that you be willing to step back from. It is perfectly wonderful to accept feelings of joy when they occur without pairing it with fear that the other shoe will drop simply because you were present in your feelings of being joyful. Why do we do that to ourselves? It's actually scary to allow ourselves to feel happy and experience true joy! Each time you feel the two (happiness and joy), stop for a moment and give yourself permission to trust that it doesn't mean that catastrophe is around the corner. Ride the high waves as long as they exist and enjoy them while you can. Life is life and the waves will ebb and flow. They will come down but not because you felt joy. When they come down, it's a natural cycle of life.

This is important to note because until you break free from this pattern, nothing will really change or free up. It's safe to say that just about everyone does it. We are conditioned to. There are many behaviors that are damaging that come with the conditioning we have been programmed to follow. When you feel joy, allow yourself the freedom to feel it! Welcome it! Savor it! It came to you for a reason. Sit with it. Be present in it. Stay present for as long as it sticks around. I mentioned earlier that the goal is to be able to sit within the discomforts and allow the discomforts to rise without feeling the need to remove yourself from them. Believe it or not, learning to be able to sit within the excitement and the joy can be even more difficult! Allowing all the freedom and happiness and joyful expressions to present themselves from inside yourself can be very overwhelming. We are not conditioned to accept freedom from our fears and pains. That can be considered a bold move on your part, and I for one want to see you rise to that occasion.

Think of joy as an actual prescription for health and vitality. Joy can come from so many places, and the more you know how this emotion feels inside your body, the more you will seek it out. Become daring and bold, and dare your body and your mind to be able to sit still when the freedoms rise. You are worthy of experiencing joy with reckless abandon.

Meditation Tips

You will find that for the fabulous four emotions, the meditations and the journaling are again similar to those for the heavy four. This is for consistency, allowing the body to learn new patterns of acceptance. Please approach each meditation practice as if it is new, even when you have begun to familiarize yourself with the pattern.

Be sure to use the bathroom before beginning this practice. Each practice will take approximately 15 to 20 minutes to complete. Lie down in a place where you will be comfortable and not distracted. Turn down the lights, preferably having only natural light in the room. Lie down either on the floor, a couch, or a bed. If you prefer to be seated, this works as well. Be sure you are wearing nonrestrictive clothing.

We will relax every part of the external body. Then we will relax deeper into the organs through auto-suggestion and begin the process of doing the body scan and working with each individual flower from the carrot. Keep in mind that we only work with one carrot bloom per meditation practice. I encourage you to return to the same meditation over and over until you feel the effects from every flower bloom that was planted. Continue with this practice until you feel that every available emotion has multiplied as much as it possibly can before moving on to the next set of positive emotions. You can fill out the journal and mark on the body as you repeat each practice.

Once you are finished with the meditation, you will document where you found this particular carrot bloom on your body. You will document the location of the carrot as well as where you planted the new bloom. I also ask that you record the name that you gave each carrot bloom so that you are able to recall what memory went with what practice. Remember to go to www.emilyafrancisbooks.com and click on the audio link to receive the meditation.

Audio and Written Meditation

Allow your legs to relax and your feet to fall naturally to each side. Bring your arms out slightly from the body and have the palms facing up. Allow your arms and your legs to be far enough from the centerline of your body that they can comfortably lie straight without tension. Allow your arms and legs to hang like the limbs of a rag doll. Notice that they are beginning to feel heavy and limp. Feel your spine lengthen and become heavy on the surface beneath you. Roll your head from side to side and then settle comfortably in the middle. Exhale all the breath from your body. Now take a slow, comfortable, full breath in through the nose, and exhale completely through the mouth. Make the sound *ahhh* on just the first deep release to signal to the nervous system that it is time to relax. Breathe in, 1 . . . 2 . . . 3 . . . 4 . . . Hold the breath without tension in your body. Exhale, 1 . . . 2 . . . 3 . . . 4 . . . 5 . . . 6 . . . 7 . . . 8 . . . Hold that space, having your breath fully released before inhaling again. Slow the breathing and allow the breath to set the tone for your relaxation.

Begin with your feet and tighten them by pointing and flexing them up and down slowly to the rhythm of your breath. Relax your feet. Relax your shins and calf muscles. Allow your knees to soften. Feel the tops of your thighs and the back sides of the legs relax. Inhale and hold your breath now. Tighten every single part of your legs and feet and lift your feet one inch off the surface beneath you. Exhale and allow your legs and feet to drop. Slowly inhale and clench your buttocks, then lift your buttocks and hips off the surface beneath you. Hold your breath as you lift up and tighten the muscles. Exhale, and slowly lower down and tuck your hips under you, allowing your lower back to lie flat on the surface beneath you. Inhale and hold your breath, arch your back, and lift your entire middle and upper back off the surface beneath you. Exhale and slowly lower down. Inhale and lift your shoulders up toward your ears. Hold your breath as your shoulders are raised as high as they can go. Exhale and lower your shoulders down. Inhale and hold the breath. Tighten your arms and make a fist with your hands. Lift your arms and hands one inch off the surface beneath you. Exhale and feel the heat and heaviness unwind from the tops of your shoulders, down your upper arms, around the elbows, the forearms and wrists, into the palms of your hands, and off each fingertip as you lower your arms down and relax your hands. Inhale and hold your breath. Squeeze your face, tighten your eyelids, and clench your jaw. Exhale and relax your face. Inhale and hold your breath for a moment. Exhale and open your mouth, stick your tongue out as far as you can, open your eyes wide, and try to bring your eyebrows up to the top of your hairline. As you stick your tongue out and exhale, make the *ahhh* sound again, signaling to your central nervous system to relax and let go. Once you have released the final audible exhalation, gently relax your entire face. Relax your ears. Relax your scalp and every hair on your head. Breathe slowly and deeply without pressure. Gently bring your awareness all the way up and down your entire physical body making sure that every part of your body is completely and entirely relaxed.

Allow your mind only to wander deeper into your body now. We will proceed to relax the organs of the body by using an auto-suggestion to relax our organs. Repeat in your mind after me:

I am relaxing my entire body. My body is relaxing. My body is relaxed.

I am relaxing my bladder. My bladder is relaxing. My bladder is relaxed.

I am relaxing the reproductive organs of my body. My reproductive organs are relaxing. My reproductive organs are relaxed.

I am relaxing my small and large intestines. My intestines are relaxing. My intestines are relaxed.

I am relaxing my stomach and pancreas. My stomach and pancreas are relaxing. My stomach and pancreas are relaxed.

I am relaxing my spleen. My spleen is relaxing. My spleen is relaxed.

I am relaxing my liver and my gallbladder. My liver and gallbladder are relaxing. My liver and gallbladder are relaxed.

I am relaxing my kidneys and my adrenal glands. My kidneys and adrenal glands are relaxing. My kidneys and adrenal glands are relaxed.

I am relaxing my lungs. My lungs are relaxing. My lungs are relaxed.

I am relaxing my heart. My heart is relaxing. My heart is relaxed.

I am relaxing my brain. My brain is relaxing. My brain is relaxed.

I am relaxing all the organs in my body. All my organs are relaxing. All my organs are relaxed.

I am relaxing my mind. I am slowing down my thoughts. I am calming down my feelings. My mind is deeply and completely relaxed.

I am relaxing my entire body. My entire body is relaxing. My entire body is relaxed.

Now bring your awareness into the deepest, darkest, most hidden parts of your body. Go into the bloodstream now and gently surf through your body inside the blood and plasma. Use this liquid flow to guide you throughout your entire body one full time. Become an observer of the way in which your body flows beneath the surface. Bring yourself into the darkness where the master factory of the muscles, fasciae, and other soft tissues are at work keeping you alive and healthy. Once you have scanned and surfed through your own flow of movement within, allow your eyes to turn inward and go anywhere that your body asks you to go. We begin to scan the entire body all the way from the top of the head to the bottoms of the feet. Now go deeper into the layer that is almost never seen, into your sacred garden. All we can see is deep, dark soil laid out through every channel of our body. This is the deepest layer of our being where only the garden lives. Within the soil are rows of carrots. We are scanning the garden for carrots that have green tops and flower blossoms growing above the green bunch of the carrot. The flower blooms are usually white in color but can have light hues of various pastel colors. These flowers have bloomed from the carrots that were implanted in your body because of emotions that came from happy and loving experiences.

Look closely as you begin to notice very small blossoms of soft-colored flowers growing just above the surface. Discover your garden however you like, whether by walking slowly up and down the lines of the soil, scanning with your eyes, using your sense of smell for something light and fragrant, or gently moving your hands across the soil in search of soft flowers grown from the tops of the carrots. It is your practice and your choice on how to connect deeply with the spaces where you have planted a harvest. We set our intention in this deep space that our body opens up to us and unites with our consciousness for our greatest good and strongest health now. The messages of the body are subtle, and you must be open to receive them. In this space we are able to gently pull a few of the blooms and replant them in other areas of the body to increase the positive emotions throughout.

Think of the word ***joy***. We now open ourselves up to any messages, images, or flashes of light or color that catch our eye to what comes with the thought of *joy*. Notice when that word enters your consciousness that one flash of color will light up from somewhere deep inside your inner garden. Look for the soft blooms of lighter and more loving life experiences of *joy* during various times of your life. Notice now that one of the flower blooms has alerted you to its presence. Bring all your awareness to this one carrot. In your mind's eye, imagine a tiny version of yourself going next to this carrot and sitting down beside it. None of this should be approached quickly. Each carrot has planted itself into the area and grown deep roots from the time of its inception. Be gentle as you look, listen, and ask this carrot to tell you how it got there. Allow the carrot that represents this first round of *joy* to tell you its story. Not your story. Not the story that you have been telling yourself all this time. Allow the emotion from the *joyful* times to wash over you and bring you back into that space as it shares images and feelings with you from that time in your life. Bask in this moment to relive it again, as if it is happening in real time. Maybe people whom you have loved and lost show up in these images. Maybe it is something with just yourself. Whatever stories are shared come from the flower that bloomed because of the experience. Be grateful, but do not get ahead of your thoughts. Let the flower tell you its story and take you back in time with it.

Once it shares with you an image or an actual story, feel free to name that flower. Name it something to ensure that its story is heard, that you understand its meaning, and that you are thankful to be reminded of it. Ask the carrot, by its new name, if it would be all right if you pulled out just a few of the blooms in order to plant them in other parts of your body for increased *joy*, health, and love. Once you feel the carrot has given you permission to pull out and plant the flower blooms, see yourself taking one hand and gently pinching off those blooms to replant elsewhere. These are the blooms that embraced life fully, that allowed you to truly enjoy the feeling of *joy*. Embrace the sensations as they wash over you and remind you just how sweet and pleasant life can be. This is your life! It is yours to make new in this moment and to begin again by planting a bountiful harvest that you have sowed in your life.

Place a single word of intention into this area to grow and radiate out into your body. What do you hope for in feeling the refreshing laughter and love and health and healing from *joy*? Now take the carrot blossom and plant it in another part of your body that needs love and healing. Affirm that it will now grow new roots and help you heal yourself from within. Gently smile and feel the power of intention in your healing. Be sure to give thanks to both the carrot with the flower and the newly planted blooms. Breathe deeply into this space, and when you are ready, take your awareness back up a few layers, until you can feel the air on your skin. Breathe slowly and deeply and keep your eyes closed until the very end. Gently begin to wiggle your fingers and your toes. Notice the air becoming cooler with each breath. Feel the air on your skin and bring your awareness back into the room and now fully into your external body. When you are ready and with a renewed sense of purpose and light, open your eyes and return, return, return.

Journal

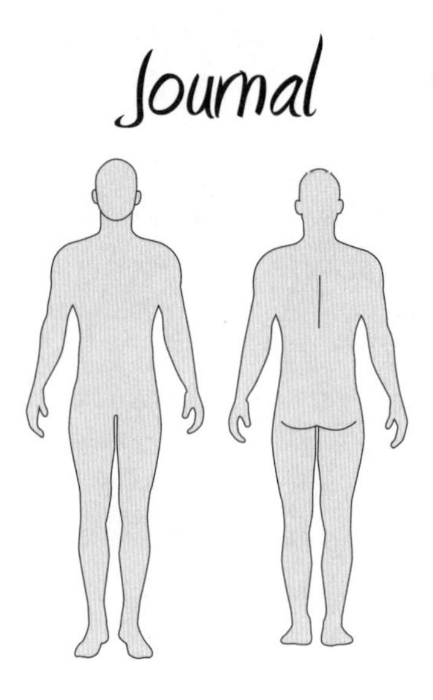

Joy

What wild carrot bloom presented itself to you when you meditated on the concept of feeling joy?

___

Where was that carrot bloom located in the body?

___

How did it show itself to you?

___

What was the story that the carrot shared with you?

___

How did it make you feel when you experienced it again?

___

How was it different from the story that you identify with in that particular circumstance?

___

Did you learn anything from what the carrot had to share with you?

___

What did the flowers look like? What color were they?

___

___

What name did you give to the bloom for this story?

___

Where did you plant the new bloom in your body, and why did you choose that place?

___

How do you feel in your body now after planting flowers in other areas of the body?

___

What follow-up practices do you intend to do in order to continue with the new loving space in your body? (Examples include counseling, therapy, writing a letter, placing your hand over that place in your body coupled with an affirmation allowing that new healing to remain, writing how you feel and putting it up on your mirror or someplace where you can see it daily, etc.) Make a commitment now to follow through with this work to be sure that the new blooms are committed to growing and multiplying in your body.

Repeat the following affirmation: *I deserve all the happiness, joy, light, love, and radiant health that are coming to me now. I am happy. I am joyful. I am healthy. I am strong. I am healing.*

Pairing the Affirmation with a Hand Position or Mudra

When we create an affirmation to repeat following our deep meditation work, it is important that we also pair the practice with a specific touch to fully activate and align both the tissue memory patterns and the mental groove sets. There are many options to help dialogue deeply with our bodies. Feel free to explore all these suggestions and choose which of these works best for you and your specific work.

The two-hand touch involves placing your left middle fingertip directly over the navel. The left hand is the receiving hand. In Chinese medicine, this is the CV8 point. The CV8 translates to the "spirit gate." This is a point of integration to help recalibrate your current energy to match "the vibrational remedy that is placed upon it."[12] Place the right middle fingertip on the top of the head directly at the midline. The right hand is considered the giving hand. This point in Chinese medicine is known as the *baijiu* or the DU20 point. This point translates to "the meeting of the hundreds." It is the place where all the energies within the body "converge and meet."[13]

The specific point to be aware of is the spot where we first touch the tips of the ears and meet our fingers together at the top of the head. In or around that area will be an incredibly slight dip in that suture line. That is the spot to touch. Once you find it, you'll be able to locate it with ease moving forward.

Prayer hands is the most notable hand position or mudra known worldwide to prepare and activate our connection to the heavens as well as to activate the clearing of the mind and the opening of the heart space. Prayer hands asks that God enter our work and help us to clear and heal.

Mudras include touching together specific fingers to activate a certain energy and intention. The most basic hand mudra besides prayer hands is to connect the first finger to the thumb (chin mudra) to connect yourself with the universe. The index finger represents you, and the thumb represents the universe. How you naturally place the two fingers together can give insight into where you are in relation with the universe. Tucking the finger under the thumb indicates that you are bowing down to the universe. Meeting tip to tip would indicate that you feel even with the universe: not above or beneath the energy itself.

Chapter 10
Connected

Being *connected* occurs when you've learned the experiences of feeling happy and then go deeper into the joy cycle. Once these build on each other, something shifts inside the body and begins to form a connection among the memory tracks. Imagine for a moment that every cell in your body is magnetically charged. I'm not saying this is fact or fiction; just imagine that each cell is shaped like a tube and on each end is either a positive or negative charge. When we are disconnected, the cells' ends do not attract but instead are mismatched. Some are attracted and connect to one another, while others are completely disconnected, with a force that repels one end of the cell away from the next cell. All our cells move like a highway system, and our cells are utterly chaotic when they don't match up and work together as an integrated system. Imagine a traffic jam of sideways cells and repelling cells and attaching cells, and there is no rhyme or reason to the madness!

That is what it's like in the cellular system, the memory systems, the whole soft tissue system of the body when we are disconnected. This is where the disconnect, or the dis-ease, can stem from. We may not have even been aware that our systems have been semi-functioning in chaos for the majority of our lives until the moment finally comes when we guide the cells within our bodies for all parts to come together on the same page for the sake of our healing and recovery. The cells then figure it out and line up, positive charges following negative ones, attracting one another and able to form lines to move about within our blood, plasma, and tissue flow. Imagine the amazing benefits if our bodies and our minds would feel and function as if everything was meant to get to the same single-pointed focus and execution behind our well-being. Remember my friend, in the Introduction, who looked me in the eyes and vowed to set off a chain reaction to ensure that sweet Belle the dog would never return to her old dysfunctional yard again? This is finally our moment to bring it all home. This is your time to focus on a single point that takes from the outside in and the inside out to set off the chain of command within our operating systems to work together harmoniously. Here the miracles can be discovered and reversals in health and wellness can be born.

Homeostasis is the term that refers to our natural state of balance. Our body is always attempting to achieve homeostasis. Finally, in this space it is achieved! We are in a state of balance! We are in a state where there are no dissenting votes on the board of trustees within our body's communications board! Can you begin to imagine what that might look like? Can you imagine how that might feel? That is the profound state of somatic connectedness. This is the place of bliss where everything starts to fall into place for us. We begin to feel healthy, and we in turn begin to act in ways that perpetuate that state of healthy. We are not in a place of self-sabotaging or testing our own resolve to see how we would manage another jungle of overload. When we are in a state of balance, it is natural to do everything we can to maintain that state of balance. We begin to crave the healthy foods, healthy mindset, exercise, and breathing with intention and with gratitude, searching for deeper meaning and making our lives more purposeful. When we are in a state of imbalance, our bodies tend to crave the things that keep us off balance. It's what we know. But once you know the experience of connectedness within your body, mind, and soul, you will follow the path to keep it. Choose to level up right now in this space. Enter this meditation work for connectedness within your body and begin to lay the new tracks down. You can do this. You will thank yourself for doing this.

When we discuss the idea of the somatic chart and say that the concept of being connected is almost the highest on the ladder of the fabulous four, this is why. When we become connected within every fiber of our beings—body, mind, and spirit—our whole world begins to change in the most glorious ways. Being connected is entirely about what is happening within our systems. Every system feels safe, healthy, and in glorious working order where supreme health comes alive and begins to be the captain of your vessel. The hardest part is not to second-guess it, not to go out of your way to try to jinx it or mess it up for yourself. Burn the bridge between you and self-sabotaging behaviors. This is the space you can finally come to where you accept and allow real healing and happiness to enter into your life. Not just to enter, but to be the lead role of your life! This is the time when trust begins to play a part and you get to the place of trusting your journey into creating a reality for yourself that is rooted in vitality, trust, connection, peacefulness, acceptance, clearing of the old pains, and planting of the new pleasures. Connecting allows you to tap into a different flow of life. Just like there are energy cords, there are also various energy flows. How is it that some people seem so in sync when others seem constantly discombobulated? We make a choice to decide which flow we want to surf through in our lives. Those flows don't even present to us until we realize that they are real. I personally believe that there are lots of different flows that are options for each of us. When we are not in the right place, it can feel like living inside the wrong flow. We know there is something better out there, but we have no idea how to jump from where we are to hop on to a flow that provides comfort and excitement in life. Getting here allows you to finally achieve the highest and smoothest flow of life that was always meant for you.

We have seen people who are living their best life. We've probably wondered how they got there. This is one of the options. You deserve all the most wonderful offerings that life has to give. You are no less or no more than any other human being on this planet. Free will to choose your path is based on every best step that you take once you become conscious that you are in charge of the life you lead. Obviously, you don't have every choice, because there is a higher power that created you, and you don't get to know all the answers while you are here. But we are not here just blindly accepting whatever life throws at us. Maybe it's time to stop living our lives on the defense and change sides to the offense. Set the path to get to your destination. Set your intentions, go for it all the way, and follow it through. You are enough. You deserve this chance to set the patterns inside and outside to the highest setting possible. This is part of being human. You have choices. Free will is a true reality. Start to use it for your greater good. At every single moment, we are presented with choices. Turn left or right, move up or back. Accept that we can achieve great things, and take the follow-up steps to bring it to life or sit down and watch our opportunities go by. These are choices. Once you connect inside yourself, I promise you that your outside life will line up, too. New opportunities will present themselves. As long as you stay connected within yourself, you will begin to trust your path and your process. You will also realize that life was not always out to get you. The value that you place on your life and the understanding of the amazing opportunities will not be lost on you. Be connected, and get on the same team of intention for your health, for your life, for your dreams, and for your ability to reach those goals! You can do anything you set your mind to and follow through on. Being connected offers the change to finally start to believe that this is true for you!

Meditation Tips

You will find that for the fabulous four emotions, the meditation and the journaling are again similar to those for the heavy four. This is for consistency in allowing the body to learn new patterns of acceptance. Please approach each meditation practice as if it is new, even when you begin to familiarize yourself with the pattern.

Be sure to use the bathroom before beginning this practice. Each practice will take approximately 15 to 20 minutes to complete. Lie down in a place where you will be comfortable and not distracted. Turn down the lights, preferably having only natural light in the room. Lie down either on the floor, a couch, or a bed. If you prefer to be seated, this works as well. Be sure you are wearing nonrestrictive clothing.

We will relax every part of the external body. Then we will relax deeper into the organs through auto-suggestion and then begin the process of doing the body scan and working with each individual budding flower from the carrot. Keep in mind that we work with only one carrot bloom per meditation practice. I encourage you to return to the same meditation over and over until you feel the effects from every flower bloom that was planted. Continue with this practice until you feel that every available emotion has multiplied as much as it possibly can before moving on to the next set of positive emotions. You can fill out the journal and mark on the body as you repeat each practice.

Once you are finished with the meditation, you will document where you found this particular carrot bloom in the body. You will also document the location of the carrot as well as where you planted the new bloom. I also ask that you record the name that you gave each carrot bloom so that you are able to recall what memory went with what practice. Remember to go to www.emilyafrancisbooks.com and click on the audio link to receive the meditation.

Audio and Written Meditation

Allow your legs to relax and your feet to fall out naturally to each side. Bring your arms out slightly from the body and have the palms facing up. Allow your arms and your legs to be far enough from the center line of your body that they can comfortably lie straight without tension. Allow your arms and legs to hang like the limbs of a rag doll. Notice that they are beginning to feel heavy and limp. Feel your spine straighten and become heavy on the surface beneath you. Roll your head from side to side and then settle comfortably in the middle. Exhale all the breath from your body first. Now take a slow, comfortable, full breath in through your nose, and exhale completely through your mouth. Make the sound *ahhh* on the first deep release to signal to the nervous system that it is time to relax. Breathe in, 1 . . . 2 . . . 3 . . . 4 . . . Hold the breath without tension in your body. Exhale, 1 . . . 2 . . . 3 . . . 4 . . . 5 . . . 6 . . . 7 . . . 8 . . . Hold that space, having your breath fully released before inhaling again. Slow your breathing and allow the breath to set the tone for your relaxation.

Beginning with your feet, tighten them by pointing and flexing your feet up and down slowly to the rhythm of your breath. Relax your feet. Relax your shins and calf muscles. Allow your knees to soften. Feel the tops of your thighs and the back sides of your legs relax. Inhale and hold your breath now. Tighten every single part of your legs and feet and lift your feet one inch off the surface beneath you. Exhale and allow your legs and feet to drop. Slowly inhale and clench your buttocks, then lift your buttocks and hips off the surface beneath you. Hold your breath as you lift up and tighten the muscles. Exhale, and slowly lower down and tuck your hips under you, allowing your lower back to lie flat on the surface beneath you. Inhale and hold your breath, arch your back, and lift your entire middle and upper back off the surface beneath you. Exhale and slowly lower yourself back down. Inhale and lift your shoulders up toward your ears. Hold your breath as your shoulders are raised as high as they can go. Exhale and lower your shoulders down. Inhale and hold the breath. Tighten your arms and make a fist with your hands. Lift your arms and hands one inch off the surface beneath you. Exhale and feel the heat and heaviness unwind from the tops of your shoulders, down the upper arms, around the elbows, the forearms and wrists, into the palms of your hands, and off each fingertip as you lower your arms down and relax your hands. Inhale and hold your breath. Squeeze your face, tighten your eyelids, and clench your jaw. Exhale and relax your face. Inhale and hold your breath for a moment. Exhale and open your mouth, stick your tongue out as far as you can, open your eyes wide, and try to bring your eyebrows up to the top of your hairline. As you stick your tongue out and exhale, make the *ahhh* sound again, signaling to your central nervous system to relax and let go. Once you have released the final audible exhalation, gently relax your entire face. Relax your ears. Relax your scalp and every hair on your head. Breathe slowly and deeply without pressure. Gently bring your awareness all the way up and down your entire physical body, making sure that every part of your body is completely and entirely relaxed.

Allow your mind only to wander deeper into your body now. We will proceed to relax the organs of the body by using an auto-suggestion. Repeat in your mind after me:

I am relaxing my entire body. My body is relaxing. My body is relaxed.

I am relaxing my bladder. My bladder is relaxing. My bladder is relaxed.

I am relaxing the reproductive organs of my body. My reproductive organs are relaxing. My reproductive organs are relaxed.

I am relaxing my small and large intestines. My intestines are relaxing. My intestines are relaxed.

I am relaxing my stomach and pancreas. My stomach and pancreas are relaxing. My stomach and pancreas are relaxed.

I am relaxing my spleen. My spleen is relaxing. My spleen is relaxed.

I am relaxing my liver and my gallbladder. My liver and gallbladder are relaxing. My liver and gallbladder are relaxed.

I am relaxing my kidneys and my adrenal glands. My kidneys and adrenal glands are relaxing. My kidneys and adrenal glands are relaxed.

I am relaxing my lungs. My lungs are relaxing. My lungs are relaxed.

I am relaxing my heart. My heart is relaxing. My heart is relaxed.

I am relaxing my brain. My brain is relaxing. My brain is relaxed.

I am relaxing all the organs in my body. All my organs are relaxing. All my organs are relaxed.

I am relaxing my mind. I am slowing down my thoughts. I am calming down my feelings. My mind is deeply and completely relaxed.

I am relaxing my entire body. My entire body is relaxing. My entire body is relaxed.

Now bring your awareness into the deepest, darkest, most hidden parts of your body. Go into the bloodstream now and gently surf through your body inside the blood and plasma. Use this liquid flow to guide you throughout your entire body one full time. Become an observer of the way in which your body flows beneath the surface. Bring yourself into the darkness where the master factory of the muscles, fasciae, and other soft tissues are at work, keeping you alive and healthy. Once you have scanned and surfed through your own flow of movement within, allow your eyes to turn inward and go anywhere that your body asks you to go. We begin to scan the entire body, all the way from the top of the head to the bottoms of the feet. Now go deeper into the layer that is almost never seen, into your sacred garden. All we can see is deep, dark soil laid out through every channel of your body. This is the deepest layer of our being where only the garden lives. Within the soil are rows of carrots. We are scanning the garden for carrots that have the green tops and flower blossoms growing above the green bunch of the carrot. The flower blooms are usually white but can have light hues of various pastel colors. These flowers have bloomed from the carrots that were implanted into your body because of emotions that were happy and loving experiences.

Look closely as you begin to notice very small soft-colored flower blossoms growing just above the surface of the carrots. Discover your garden however you like, whether by walking slowly up and down the lines of the soil, scanning with your eyes, using your sense of smell for something light and fragrant, or gently moving your hands across the body soil in search of soft flowers grown from the tops of the carrots. It is your practice and your choice on how to connect deeply into the spaces where you have planted a harvest. We set our intentions in this deep space that our body opens up to us and unites with our consciousness for our greatest good and strongest health. The messages of the body are subtle, and you must be open to receive them. In this space, we are able to gently pull a few of the blooms and replant them in other areas of the body in order to increase the positive emotions throughout.

Think of the word ***connected.*** We now open ourselves up to any messages, images, or flashes of light or color that catch our eye to what comes with the thought of being *connected*. Notice when that word enters your consciousness that one flash of color will light up from somewhere deep inside your inner garden. Look for the soft blooms of lighter and more loving life experiences of feeling *connected* during various times of your life. Notice now that one of the flowers has alerted you to its presence. Bring all your awareness to this one carrot. In your mind's eye, imagine a tiny version of your whole self going next to this carrot and sitting down beside it. None of this should be approached quickly. Each carrot has planted itself into the area and grown deep roots from the time of its inception. Be gentle as you look, listen, and ask this carrot to tell you how it got there. Allow the carrot that represents this first round of feeling *connected* to tell you its story. Not your story. Not the story that you have been telling yourself all this time. Allow the emotion from the *connected* times to wash over you and bring you back into that space as it shares images and feelings with you from that time in your life. Bask in this moment to relive it again as if it is happening in real time. Maybe people whom you have loved and lost show up in these images. Maybe it is something that involves only yourself. Whatever stories are shared are from the flower that bloomed because of the experience. Be grateful, but do not get ahead of your thoughts. Let the flower tell you its story and take you back in time with it.

Once it shares with you an image or an actual story, feel free to name that carrot. Name it something to ensure that its story is heard, that you understand its meaning, and that you are thankful to be reminded of it. Ask the carrot, by its new name, if it would be all right if you pulled out just a few of the blooms in order to plant them in other parts of your body for increased *connection,* health, and love. Once you feel the carrot has given you permission to pull them out and plant them, see yourself taking one hand and gently pinching off those blooms to replant elsewhere. These are the blooms that embraced life fully, that allowed you to truly enjoy the feeling of being *connected.* Embrace the sensations as they wash over you and remind you just how sweet and pleasant life can be. This is your life! It is yours to make new in this moment, and to begin again by planting a bountiful harvest.

Place a single word of intention into this area to grow and radiate out into your body. What do you hope for in feeling the refreshing laughter and love and health and healing from feeling *connected*? Now place the bloom that you have gently pinched off from that one carrot and plant it in another part of your body that needs love and healing. Affirm that those blooms will now grow new roots and help you heal yourself from within. Gently smile and feel the power of intention in your healing. Be sure to give thanks to both the carrot with the flower and the newly planted blooms. Breathe deeply into this space, and when you are ready, take your awareness back up a few layers until you can feel the air on your skin. Breathe slowly and deeply and keep your eyes closed until the very end. Gently begin to wiggle your fingers and your toes. Notice the air becoming cooler with each breath. Feel the air on your skin and bring your awareness back into the room and now fully into your external body. When you are ready and with a renewed sense of purpose and light, open your eyes and return, return, return.

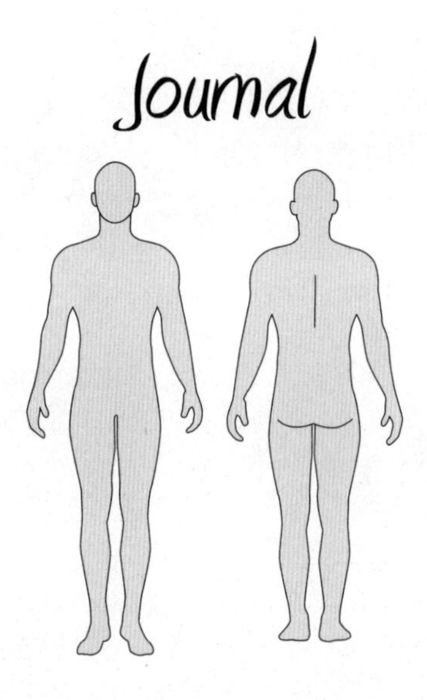

Connected

What was the wild carrot bloom that presented itself to you when you meditated on the concept of feeling connected?

____

Where was that carrot bloom located in the body?

____

How did it show itself to you?

____

What was the story that the carrot shared with you?

____

How did it make you feel when you experienced it again?

____

How was it different from the story that you identify with in that particular circumstance?

____

Did you learn anything from what the carrot had to share with you?

____

What did the flowers look like? What color were they?

____

What name did you give to the bloom for this story?

____

Where did you plant the new bloom in your body, and why did you choose that place?

____

How do you feel in your body now after planting blooms in other areas of the body?

____

What follow-up practices do you intend to do in order to continue with the new loving space in your body? (Examples include counseling, writing it a letter, placing your hand over that place in your body coupled with an affirmation allowing that new healing to remain, writing how you feel and putting it on your mirror or someplace where you can see it daily, etc.) Make a commitment now to follow through with this work to be sure that the new blooms are committed to growing and multiplying in your body.

Repeat the following affirmation: *I deserve all the happiness, joy, connections, light, love, and radiant health that are coming to me now. I am happy. I am joyful. I feel connected. I am healthy. I am strong. I am healing.*

Pairing the Affirmation with a Hand Position or Mudra

When we create an affirmation to repeat following our deep meditation work, it is important that we also pair the practice with a specific touch to the body to fully activate and align the tissue memory patterns along with the mental groove sets. There are many options to dialogue deeply with the body. Feel free to explore all these suggestions and choose which of these works best for you and your specific work.

The two-hand touch involves placing the left middle fingertip directly over the navel. The left hand is the receiving hand. In Chinese medicine this is the CV8 point. The CV8 translates to the "spirit gate." This is a point of integration to help recalibrate your current energy to match "the vibrational remedy that is placed upon it."[12] Place the right middle fingertip on the top of the head directly at the midline. The right hand is considered the giving hand. This point in Chinese medicine is known as the *baijiu* or the DU20 point. This point translates to "the meeting of the hundreds." It is the place where all the energies within the body "converge and meet."[13]

The specific point to be aware of is the spot where we first touch the tips of the ears and meet our fingers together at the top of the head. In or around that area will be an incredibly slight dip in that suture line. That is the spot to touch. Once you find it, you'll be able to locate it with ease moving forward.

Prayer hands is the most notable hand position or mudra known worldwide to prepare and activate our connection to the heavens as well as to activate the clearing of the mind and the opening of the heart space. Prayer hands asks that God enter our work and help us to clear and heal.

Mudras include touching together specific fingers to activate a certain energy and intention. The most basic hand mudra besides prayer hands is to connect the first finger to the thumb (chin mudra) to connect yourself with the universe. The index finger represents you, and the thumb represents the universe. How you naturally place the two fingers together can give insight into where you are with the universe. Tucking the finger under the thumb indicates that you are bowing down to the universe. Meeting tip to tip would indicate that you feel even with the universe: not above or beneath the energy itself.

Chapter 11

Empowered

Being connected pulls you into your own full-blast achievement, in which all the body systems work together for your greatest good and the highest joys come to fruition in your life. Once you feel connected within yourself, you can finally assimilate this both inside of yourself and outside of yourself. This work incorporates all of life that surrounds you. It is a grounding power that comes from within but is now expanding out into the world! Becoming empowered is something so powerful, so sacred, so unique, and so achievable once you get to this level that you will possibly wonder where you have been all your life! You are the sexiest, strongest, most supple highlight of your own life! You become everything that you've been looking for outside yourself for so long and now here you are! Becoming empowered implies that you begin to fully come to the place where you trust yourself, your life, and the plan God has for you in your life, and you finally start to live up to it. Not because of anyone else, of course, and not for anyone else. This is now about you. Repeat the affirmation: ***I choose me!*** The happy, joyful, connected, and empowered *you*! You finally realize that all the outside influences, the numbers on any scale, the concept of what others want you to be, what others have expected you to be, that all seems to lighten up and float away. Your life becomes exactly that: *your life*. You have removed your carrots, replaced every bit of trauma, shame, and guilt with love, and rearranged the patterns from how you dealt with those from your past. You have put grief into a place of acceptance, and though grief never goes away, it can be rearranged so that you can live with certain losses and still allow yourself to feel happy moving forward, too. You realize you are not bad, and you don't deserve to be punished anymore for any of the past. You have moved across the action bridge and faced the hardest days, replaced the pains, and cut ties with the deep trauma and pain, shame and guilt. You have allowed yourself to release the things that held you down and made you a prisoner to your own life. You have moved yourself through understanding what it feels like to be happy. You've gone deeper into the experiences of true joy and allowed yourself the opportunity to feel both without creating a false sense of punishment for feeling the good things. You've been reminded of the way that the memory systems within your body operate when they feel healthy and happy. You've used those wonderful feelings to build more of the same within yourself. You've elevated without realizing just how much you've already risen. Becoming connected internally is so incredibly and subtly powerful. There is not much that feels as blissful to the internal body as finally getting it together and working as a full team for your health and vitality.

You have become fully empowered in your own beautiful and glorious self and can take this new connectedness and joy out into the world with you. Being empowered comes with every step you take and every decision that you choose to make. It widens the mind and expands your perception of life and how you expand within it. It goes with you everywhere that you go. It becomes who you are. You are able to fully hold your own space and not just feel comfortable in it, but embody everything incredible that you have ever seen in someone else. It is a deep-rootedness into the earth, and at the same time, a powerful connection into the heavens. You take full power over the life that God has given you.

You finally understand that you are allowed to accept that you deserve all good things, and you want to see yourself create more. You may also choose to help to empower others from this new space. You (hopefully) will become less self-serving and see the bigger picture in all things and the part that you play within those scenes. It is a place so much bigger than confidence. It is a rootedness and a connectedness and a foundation of finally owning your own sacred self. In turn, it allows you to see the sacredness of everyone else you meet. It creates a sense of self that allows more to roll off the back when other people act in ways that once would have triggered you. Now you realize that other people's behaviors really have nothing to do with you, so you continue living your best life without an attachment to those other people who haven't gotten there yet. You have become the fully awake and authentic version of yourself. You are no longer hiding old secrets and wounds.

One of the most difficult parts of healing is getting to the place where you forgive any parts of yourself that blocked the way before and giving yourself permission to heal and thrive. Feelings of being unworthy are deeply rooted within so many of us, and it is really a challenge to finally let them go and step into the life that you've dreamed of creating for yourself. That is the lesson in becoming empowered. You have arrived at the next phase of your life, the one that you create for yourself. This is the start of understanding that everything from here on out derives from choices you make and actions you take or choose not to take. You finally understand how to own your responsibility without so much heaviness attached to it.

You have done your personal work to allow yourself to heal from the depths within the body itself. The freedom that comes with taking off the heavy cloak of trauma/shame/guilt is liberating. All this time, we observed our life as if we were watching a movie. If you were in a movie right now, you would be walking away from the heavy cloak lying lifeless on the ground behind you. You would swiftly and gracefully walk over the bridge into bright sunlight with an angelic choir singing in the background. Your arms would be up, and your face would be smiling and facing the heavens as you embrace the new, glorious life that awaits you.

Meditation Tips

You will find that for the fabulous four emotions, the meditation and the journaling are again similar to those for the heavy four. This is for consistency in allowing the body to learn new patterns of acceptance. Please approach each meditation practice as if it is new, even when you begin to familiarize yourself with the pattern.

Be sure to use the bathroom before beginning this practice. Each practice will take approximately 15 to 20 minutes to complete. Lie down in a place where you will be comfortable and without distractions. Turn down the lights, preferably having only natural light in the room. Lie down either on the floor, a couch, or a bed. If you prefer to be seated, this works as well. Be sure you are wearing nonrestrictive clothing.

We will relax every part of the external body. We will relax deeper into the organs through auto-suggestion and then begin the process of doing the body scan and working with each individual budding flower from the carrot. Keep in mind that we work with only one single carrot bloom per meditation practice. I encourage you to return to the same meditation over and over until you feel the effects from every flower bloom that was planted. Continue with this practice until you feel that every available emotion has multiplied as much as it possibly can. You can fill out the journal and mark on the body as you repeat each practice.

Once you are finished with the meditation, you will document where you found this particular carrot bloom in the body. You will also document the location of the carrot as well as where you planted the new bloom. I also ask that you record the name that you gave each carrot bloom so that you are able to recall what memory went with what practice. Remember to go to www.emilyafrancisbooks.com and click on the audio link to receive the meditation.

Audio and Written Meditation

Allow your legs to relax and your feet to fall out naturally to each side. Bring the arms out slightly from the body and have the palms facing up. Allow your arms and your legs to be far enough from the center line of your body that they are able to comfortably lie straight without tension. Allow your arms and legs to hang like the arms and legs of a rag doll. Let your arms and legs begin to feel heavy and limp. Feel your spine straighten and become heavy to the surface beneath you. Roll your head from side to side and then settle comfortably in the middle. Exhale all the breath from your body first. Then take a slow, comfortable full breath in through the nose, and exhale completely through the mouth. Make the sound *ahhh* on just the first deep release to signal to the nervous system to relax. Breathe in following a count of 1 . . . 2 . . . 3 . . . 4 . . . and hold the breath without tension in the body. Exhale for 1 . . . 2 . . . 3 . . . 4 . . . 5 . . . 6 . . . 7 . . . 8 . . . Hold that space without the breath before inhaling again. Slow the breathing and allow the breath to set the tone for your relaxation.

Begin with your feet and tighten them by pointing and flexing them up and down slowly to the rhythm of your breath. Relax your feet. Relax your shins and calf muscles. Allow your knees to soften. Feel the tops of your thighs and the back sides of the legs relax. Inhale and hold your breath now. Tighten every single part of the legs and feet and lift your feet one inch off the surface beneath you. Exhale and allow your legs and feet to drop. Slowly inhale and clench the buttocks and lift the buttocks and hips off the surface beneath you. Hold your breath as you lift up and tighten the muscles. Exhale and slowly lower down and tuck the hips under, allowing the lower back to lie flat on the surface beneath you. Inhale and hold your breath, arch your back, and lift your entire middle and upper back off the ground. Exhale and slowly lower yourself back down. Inhale and lift the shoulders up toward your ears. Hold your breath as your shoulders raise as high as they can go. Exhale and lower the shoulders down. Inhale and hold the breath. Tighten the arms and make a fist with your hands. Lift the arms and hands one inch off the surface beneath you. Exhale and feel the heat and heaviness unwind from the tops of the shoulders down the upper arms, around the elbows, the forearms and wrists, into the palms of your hands, and off each fingertip as you lower the arms down and relax the hands. Inhale and hold your breath. Squeeze your face, tighten your eyelids, and clench your jaw. Exhale and relax your face. Inhale and hold your breath for a moment. Exhale and open your mouth, stick your tongue out as far as you can, open your eyes wide, and try to bring the eyebrows up to the top of the hairline. As you stick your tongue out and exhale, make the *ahhh* sound again, signaling to your central nervous system to relax and let go. Once you have released the final audible exhalation, gently relax your entire face. Relax your ears. Relax your scalp and every hair on your head. Breathe slowly and deeply without pressure. Gently bring your awareness all the way up and down your entire physical body, making sure that every part of your body is completely and entirely relaxed.

Allow your mind only to wander deeper into your body now. We will proceed to relax the organs of the body by using an auto-suggestion. Repeat in your mind after me:

I am relaxing my entire body. My body is relaxing. My body is relaxed.

I am relaxing my bladder. My bladder is relaxing. My bladder is relaxed.

I am relaxing all of the reproductive organs of my body. The reproductive organs are relaxing. The reproductive organs are relaxed.

I am relaxing my small and large intestines. My intestines are relaxing. My intestines are relaxed.

I am relaxing my stomach and pancreas. My stomach and pancreas are relaxing. My stomach and pancreas are relaxed.

I am relaxing my spleen. My spleen is relaxing. My spleen is relaxed.

I am relaxing my liver and my gallbladder. My liver and gallbladder are relaxing. My liver and gallbladder are relaxed.

I am relaxing my kidneys and my adrenal glands. My kidneys and my adrenal glands are relaxing. My kidneys and adrenal glands are relaxed.

I am relaxing my lungs. My lungs are relaxing. My lungs are relaxed.

I am relaxing my heart. My heart is relaxing. My heart is relaxed.

I am relaxing my brain. My brain is relaxing. My brain is relaxed.

I am relaxing all the organs in my body. All of my organs are relaxing. All my organs are relaxed.

I am relaxing my mind. I am slowing down my thoughts. I am calming down my feelings. My mind is deeply and completely relaxed.

I am relaxing my entire body. My entire body is relaxing. My entire body is relaxed.

Now bring your awareness into the deepest, darkest, most hidden parts of your body. Go into the bloodstream now and gently surf through your body inside the blood and plasma. Use this liquid flow to guide you throughout your entire body one full time. Become an observer of the way in which your body flows beneath the surface. Bring yourself into the darkness where the master factory of the muscles, fasciae, and other soft tissues are at work keeping you alive and healthy. Once you have scanned and surfed through your own flow of movement within, allow your eyes to turn inward and go anywhere that your body asks you to go. We begin to scan the entire body all the way up from the top of the head to the bottoms of the feet. Now go deeper into the layer that is almost never seen, into your sacred garden. All we can see is deep, dark soil laid out through every channel of your body. This is the deepest layer of our being where only the garden lives. Within the soil are rows of carrots. We are scanning the garden for carrots that have green tops and flower buds growing above the green bunch. The flower blooms are usually white in color but can have light hues of various pastel colors. These flowers have bloomed from the carrots that were implanted into your body because of emotions that were happy and loving experiences.

Look closely as you begin to notice very small, soft-colored flower blooms growing just above the surface. Discover your garden however you like, whether by walking slowly up and down the lines of the soil, scanning only through your eyes, using your sense of smell for something light and fragrant, or gently moving your hands across the body soil in search of soft flower blossoms grown from the tops of the carrots. It is your practice and your choice on how to connect deeply into the spaces where you have planted a harvest. We set our intentions in this deep space that our body opens up to us and unites with our consciousness for our greatest good and strongest health now. The messages of the body are subtle, and you must be open to receive its messages. In this space we are able to gently pull a few of the blooms and replant them in other areas of the body to increase the positive emotions throughout.

Think of the word ***empowered***. We now open ourselves up to any messages, images, or flashes of light or color that catches our eye with the thought of being *empowered*. Notice when that word enters your consciousness, one flash of color will light up from somewhere deep inside your inner garden. Look for the soft blooms of lighter and more loving life experiences of being *empowered* during various times of your life. Notice now that one of the flower blooms has alerted you to its presence. Bring all your awareness to this one carrot. In your mind's eye, imagine a tiny version of yourself coming next to this carrot and sitting down beside it. None of this should be approached quickly. Each carrot has planted itself into the area and grown deep roots from the time of its inception. Be gentle as you look, listen, and ask this carrot to tell you how it got there. Allow the carrot that represents this first round of feeling *empowered* to tell you its story. Not your story. Not the story that you have been telling yourself all this time. Allow the emotion from the *empowered* times to wash over you and bring you back into that space as it shares with you images and feelings from that time in your life. Bask in this moment to relive again as if it's happening in real time. Maybe people whom you have loved and lost show up in these images. Maybe it's something that involves just yourself. Whatever stories that are shared come from the flower that bloomed because of the experience. Be grateful, but do not get ahead of your thoughts. Let the flower tell you its story and take you back in time with it.

Once it shares with you an image or an actual story, feel free to name that carrot. Name it something to assure that its story is heard, that you understand its meaning, and that you are thankful to be reminded of it. Ask the carrot, by its new name, if it would be all right if you pulled out just a few of the blooms in order to plant them in other parts of your body for increased *empowerment,* health, and love. Once you feel the carrot has given you permission to pull out and plant them, see yourself taking one hand and gently pinching off those blooms to replant elsewhere. These are the blooms that embraced life fully, that allowed you to truly enjoy the feeling of being *empowered*. Embrace the sensations as they wash over you and remind you just how sweet and pleasant life can be. This is your life! It's yours to make new in this moment and to begin again by planting a bountiful harvest.

Place a single word of intention into this area to grow and radiate out into your body. What do you hope for in feeling the refreshing laughter and love and health and healing from feeling *empowered*? Now place the bloom that you have gently pinched off from that one carrot and plant it into another part of your body that needs that love and healing intention. Affirm that it will now grow new roots and help you heal yourself from within. Gently smile and feel the power of intention in your healing. Be sure to give thanks to both the carrot with the flower and the newly planted blooms. Breathe deeply into this space and when you are ready, take your awareness back up a few layers, until you can feel the air on your skin. Breathe slowly and deeply and keep your eyes closed until the very end. Gently begin to wiggle your fingers and your toes. Notice the air becoming cooler with each breath. Feel the air on your skin and bring your awareness back into the room you are lying in, and now fully into your external body. When you are ready, and with a renewed sense of purpose and light, open your eyes and return, return, return.

Journal

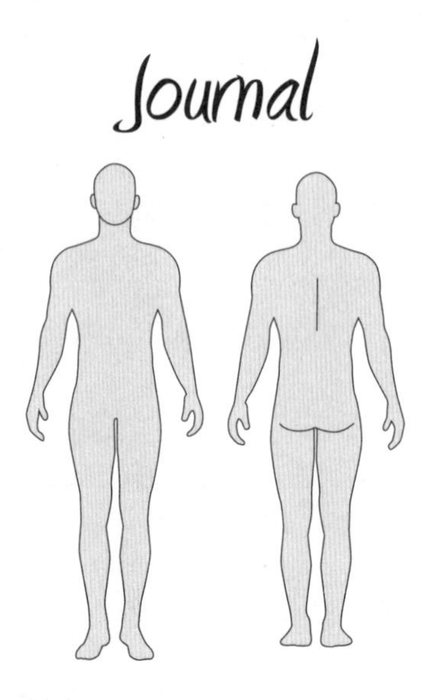

Empowered

What wild carrot bloom presented itself to you when you meditated on the concept of feeling empowered?

____

Where was that carrot bloom located in the body?

____

How did it show itself to you?

____

What was the story that the carrot shared with you?

___

How did it make you feel when you experienced it again?

___

How was it different from the story that you identify with in that particular circumstance?

___

Did you learn anything from what the carrot had to share with you?

___

What did the flowers look like? What color were they?

___

What name did you give to the carrot for this story?

___

Where did you plant the new bloom in your body, and why did you choose that place?

___

How do you feel in your body now after planting blooms in other areas of the body?

___

What follow-up practices do you intend to do in order to continue with the new loving space in your body? (Examples include counseling, writing it a letter, placing your hand over that place in your body coupled with an affirmation allowing that new healing to remain, writing how you feel and putting it on your mirror or someplace where you can see it daily, etc.) Make a commitment now to follow through with this work to be sure that the new blooms are committed to growing and multiplying in your body.

Repeat the following affirmation: *I deserve all the happiness, joy, connections, and feelings of being fully empowered that are coming to me now. I am happy. I am healthy. I am strong. I am healing.*

Pairing the Affirmation with a Hand Position or Mudra

When we create an affirmation to repeat following our deep meditation work, it is important that we also pair the practice with a specific touch to the body to fully activate and align the tissue memory patterns along with the mental groove sets. There are many options to dialogue deeply with the body. Feel free to explore all these suggestions and choose which of these work best for you and your specific work.

The two-hand touch involves placing the left middle fingertip directly over the navel. The left hand is the receiving hand. In Chinese medicine this is the CV8 point. The CV8 translates to "spirit gate." This is a point of integration to help recalibrate your current energy to match "the vibrational remedy that is placed upon it."[12] Place the right middle fingertip on the top of the head directly at the midline. The right hand is considered the giving hand. This point in Chinese medicine is known as the *baijiu* or the DU20 point. This point translates to "the meeting of the hundreds." It is the place where all the energies within the body "converge and meet."[13]

The specific point to be aware of is where we first touch the tips of the ears and meet our fingers together at the top of the head. In or around that area will be an incredibly slight dip in that suture line. That is the spot to touch. Once you find it, you'll be able to locate it with ease moving forward.

Prayer hands is the most notable hand position or mudra known worldwide to prepare and activate our connection to the heavens as well as to activate the clearing of the mind and the opening of the heart space. Prayer hands asks that God enter our work and help us to clear and heal.

Mudras include touching together specific fingers to activate a certain energy and intention. The most basic hand mudra besides prayer hands is to connect the first finger to the thumb (chin mudra) to connect yourself with the universe. The index finger represents you, and the thumb represents the universe. How you naturally place the two fingers together can give insight into where you are in relation with the universe. Tucking the finger under the thumb indicates that you are bowing down to the universe. Meeting tip to tip would indicate that you feel even with the universe: not above or beneath the energy itself.

Chapter 12

The Rebirth of You!

You're Almost Done!

Congratulations, my beautiful friend, for a fantabulous job well done! You must take time to stop and take stock on all the work that was accomplished through this practice and find out what you've learned and how far you've come for yourself. Working through the body for healing is a novel concept and one that we have overlooked for a very long time. It asks so much courage of you to take these steps and face all the old scars and secrets you've been hiding. Now that you have done all the work, you can apply these exquisite tools in your growth and healing development.

The final practice I offer to you is the opportunity for a rebirth. What if you had the chance to do your life over knowing all the things you know now? For the purpose of this work, I offer you the chance to start at the beginning and use your wisdom to give your body the strength and courage that it needed and the awareness that you are now and always were *whole*.

We will create the process of rebirthing with intentional outcomes for our life. To begin anew, we must visit the old one last time . . . but this time with a twist. Here is a secret that only those who dare to quest even understand: You are capable of healing something from the past by standing in the present. Energy travels and does not abide by the rules of time. Rules of time are Earth elements and they do not exist through any other dimension. You will create a deeper purpose to your life and give yourself love and conviction to be the person you were always destined to become. Everything you want for yourself is possible. Go back through time and remember who you were designed to be and begin again. You are about to experience a form of rebirthing that allows your present self to have a say in the life you are about to create.

Audio and Written Meditation: The Practice of Rebirthing

Be sure to use the bathroom before beginning this practice. Clear your space and remove all distractions. Turn the lights down low or off. Only allow natural light to enter this sacred space. Before lying down, bring your palms together at your heart center and ask God, the Great Spirit, the Divine (insert any words that are meaningful to you) to bring in any protectors to be present with you in this space. Ask that this practice be for the highest good and greatest joy of your soul as well as your inner child.

Lie down in a place where you will be comfortable. Close your eyes and first exhale all the air from your lungs. Next, take a slow, deep breath in through your nose and exhale fully through your mouth. Inhale through the nose . . . exhale through the mouth. Begin to follow this breathing pattern, focusing only on your breath. Deep breaths in through your nose and deeper exhalations through your mouth. Feel your stomach expand and rise as you take a breath in, then feel your stomach relax and release toward your spine as you exhale the breath out. Bring your attention to the soles of your feet and begin to breathe in through the bottoms of your feet, and then exhale, pushing any stagnant energy back down and out through the soles of the feet. Allow the breath to circle through your entire body as your physical body begins to calm and soften. Continue to repeat this breathing pattern, and now feel free to close your mouth and breathe both the inhalation and exhalation through your nose. Gently allow your mind to become calm and your thoughts to minimize naturally. Feel a circling of warm energy through your entire body, coming in through the soles of your feet, up your spine, and over your head, and exhale the breath, feeling the energy move down your face, down the center line of your body, and out through the soles of your feet. Circle with the breath around your entire being as you feel your body become heavy. Your body now feels heavy and limp and tired.

We will now separate the dense physical body and the light spirit body. In order to be fully reborn, we must be willing to travel in time. This is done only through the spirit body and not the physical body. For the purpose of this meditation, separate your light body from the physical body. As I draw this mental picture and ask you to move, do not physically move. Only do this in your mind's eye. Imagine yourself sitting on the ground with both your bottom and your feet flat on the ground with your knees bent. Feel your physical body detach itself from your thoughts now. The physical body is perfectly relaxed and comfortable, and it holds no aches or pains in this moment. Separate your body into two distinct bodies. One is your dense physical body. The other is the translucent spirit body. The physical body holds all the earthbound thoughts. The translucent body holds the heart space, the higher self, the deeper connection to the Great Spirit.

This spirit body does not have any physical density. It is light and easy. Now, move your awareness into only the translucent body. Take one step back from your physical body, turn the opposite direction, and sit back-to-back against your physical body. The body you are currently inhabiting is the light body: It is translucent and only held together by your thoughts and awareness. Stay inside that body now.

Allow your thoughts to rise higher than your physical body, staying only inside your light body. Let your light body rise up higher than your ceiling, out of your house, up to the sky, and out of the earth's orbit. Go higher and higher with each breath and thought. Begin to travel through the galaxy and notice the wide-open space that you are now traveling through. Notice if it is dark or light, if you can see stars or planets. What do you see beyond the Earth? In your mind's eye, look over to your right and notice a small vehicle parked on some sort of space pad. Go to it, open the passenger door, and get inside. Do you see the person in the driver's seat? That person is your guardian angel. The angel is here to help you do your rebirthing and to answer any questions you may have regarding your life's purpose. Simply look at the angel and say, "Thank you," for now. Let the angel take you to the moments before you were born into this life. See your soul-self just before you entered into the body of a newborn. Make eye contact as you look at yourself. What do you look like? What do you feel like? What energy do you feel from this soul before it entered into your life and became who you know to be you?

If you had this moment to do all over again, what are some of the changes you would wish to make for yourself? Are there any specific decisions or knowledge that you wish you would have known to carry into the hard times in your life? If given the opportunity of a second chance at this life, how many things would you do differently? What would you want the outcomes to be? See yourself just before you enter your Earth body. Breathe deeply into this space as you connect inside that infant body and mind. Offer the love to this child that you so desperately needed throughout your life. Offer clarity to this child. Offer opportunity to this child. Offer peace of mind and a voice of reason to this child. Offer strong health to this child. Offer unconditional love to this child.

Open one of your palms. Notice your guardian angel walk up slowly and place a small gem into the palm of your hand. Feel which palm this gem was placed in now. Take note of the color of the gem that is now in your hand. Feel the lightness and purity of this small, shiny, beautiful gem. Give thanks, and then turn back to the baby about to be born. Place the gem somewhere deep inside this child that will carry with it the recollection of the love and opportunity that you want for yourself in this life. Breathe love into the gem that you placed inside the child. Look at the gem, take a deep breath, and hold its memory for a moment. Place your lips against the jewel as you kiss the baby in that space, and with it, send all your thoughts, your intentions, your desires, your love, and your power into the gem within this child with a loud gust of an exhalation straight into the gem itself. Blow into the gem the pieces of you that you felt may have gotten lost between the time of birth and where you are now in your life. Give your infant self permission to live gracefully, happily, and boldly, with the strong conviction of who you really are. As you look at this tiny child about to enter the Earth, knowing all the things you've seen and done, take a breath in from the baby and take into yourself the innocence, the wisdom of a higher knowing, the trust, faith, and love that this untouched, unscathed little soul is carrying into the new world. Connect the energy between who you are today and who you were the moment you became human. Touch the heart space of that child and give the child all the love you can possibly muster from the deepest depths of your being. Close your eyes, merge yourself into this infant self, and take with it the gems of wisdom that you are offering to your child self now. Show that child what real, authentic, fully present love feels like so that they never forget. Look deep into the baby's eyes and allow the baby to take you with them to the pathway to becoming earth-side. Be reborn in this moment, knowing all the things you would do differently if you were given the chance to jump in and come through into this life a fully formed human being. Allow yourself to feel the birth process, coming though the birth canal and entering this plane of existence. Allow yourself to be reborn, but this time with the wisdom that can only be obtained from the life this child will live. Look to your guardian angel and know that the angel came to the other side with you, but now likely cannot be seen the way you could see them on the other side. Acknowledge the angel and commit that, from here on, you will include them in your daily life. Thank them, knowing that they will be with you, and are with you now, throughout your lifetime.

From this space, you finally understand that you were never alone in this world. There is a whole team who assists you throughout your life if you allow their help and give thanks for their assistance. Come through the birth canal within this child. Feel the first hands on you. Accept love any place you find it in the room. Find the people who love you and who loved you the most as you entered into life. Whether they are still alive or have passed, find them taking turns holding you and rocking you. Feel how it is to be in the arms of the ones you love and trust the most in the world. Experience the joy and bliss of becoming human and all the things ahead of you that you have the ability to create in your life. You are finally here! You have arrived! You are human with the chance to do it again, but this time with a gem of love and wisdom tucked away inside you to carry through this life.

Once you become human, you can separate yourself from the baby and come back into who you are now and watch your remaining birth experience from this new perspective. Feel the changes in that space from the infant into who you are currently. It does not erase pain from this part of your life, it simply protects you and offers deeper knowledge of the how and the why and the better things to come to you in your life. This offers you a renewed sense of hope and perspective that everything you want for your life is within your God-given ability to create. You have everything it takes to grow the life of your dreams for yourself.

Now think of the gem that you placed inside your soul and infant self. Where on the baby's body did you place that gem? Was it in the heart, the head, or the area of the stomach? You were offered the freedom to choose where to put that gem for a reason. The choice you made will guide you to know from which part of your body you will be able to feel the instinct and wisdom of whether you are on your best path or not. You will feel it in this particular area when you are in a good place, or if you are around anything or anyone not in alignment with your highest good. Place your own hand on the part of your current light body that holds the gem that you inserted into your infant self. Place your hands directly over that area and connect to that gem.

Develop a line of communication from your hands to that gem within you. Allow that gem to come to life and begin to work with you now to alert you to danger or to joy. Stay in this space connecting to this gem within your body until you are ready to come out of this meditation. Breathe deeply and with intention as you connect to that space within yourself that contains that little gem. Feel it come to life and know that you were able to travel in time along the spiritual dimensions in order to give yourself the best chance for your most abundantly blessed life. No matter what life threw at you, you now have the strength and stamina to work past it. You are whole. You are healthy. You feel a sense of renewal. And most of all, you are loved.

Bring your thoughts down from the galaxy, down into your home, down into the room you are in. Gently step from your light body back into your physical body and bring both bodies back together again. Mirror both sets of hands still over the gem that was placed in you. Feel the placement of that gem in both your light body and your physical body. Now, see yourself step back into your body fully. Line up the centers: spine to spine, navel to navel, nose to nose, and heart to heart. The spirit body now reenters the physical body, uniting your entire self. Feel inside you the lightness that came back into the denser physical self. Feel yourself completely connected, centered, inspired. Remember the experience of coming into this life. Make a deep conviction within yourself for the things you truly want to experience while in this body. Remain connected with that little gem inside. Are you a thinker, a feeler, a listener, or a seer? Wherever you chose to put this gem in your infant self is still the place to always connect to for clarity, information, and a confirmation of love. Never forget that you placed it inside yourself and that you are always guided. Time travel is real within the spirit realm, and the gem you placed in your infant self also lives within your adult self. Keep your eyes closed, your breath calm, and your mind clear, and be centered back into your whole body. Prepare yourself to slowly come back to the here and now and remember the information that your body gave to you.

Feel the air on your skin and the air against your nostrils as your breathing becomes present. Take your time moving your body but do give yourself a little stretch before you return.

JOURNAL

What did your guardian angel look like?

___

Did it have a name?

___

What color was the gem the angel put in your hand?

___

Where did you place that gem inside yourself?

___

The rest of this journal is blank so you can share your experiences and make notes about anything you might need to revisit through the previous chapters. It's your checkpoint station of who you were, what you've done, and where you are heading. This is a great place to be honest and create solid affirmations and intentions to move forward with.

___

___

___

___

___

___

___

Conclusion

Living Your Life on Purpose

I realize that at this point in my life, whenever I feel out of place or off my path, it is because I'm not truly living my life on purpose. I might write with purpose. I might act with purpose. But I fail sometimes to live my life truly on purpose. When we live our lives in our most true and authentic way, we climb upward. It does actually get better, and we do build on the last step we took. When we get stuck or complacent, this is not on purpose. Our lives are on autopilot and that is something totally different. The energy level is stagnant, and we can feel stuck. This is the quicksand that I talk about when our legs get heavy and our knees get angry. It's so easy to do. It's not easy to get moving again. We must constantly redefine our goals, our passions, and our hearts' truest desires and find ways to put them into action in our lives. No time to keep things only in our dreams.

Living on purpose requires you to be daring. It asks you to step outside your comfort zone and do things that you think about doing but may not have tried to do yet. Or you may have tried before and failed. Living on purpose asks you to try it again. And to keep trying.

You are worth it. Your life is worth it. Your health is worth it.

I was thinking about what I want most for my children in their lives. I find myself often praying that they live long, healthy, and happy lives. I also find myself often praying that they do something "amazing" with their lives. Then I have to ask myself, *What does amazing mean?* I don't need them to feel the pressure of having to do anything big with their lives. I don't need them to want to chase fame or fortune. I would never want to put any pressure on them to be anything but the authentic versions of themselves, which are entirely up to them to design. What I realized is that what I want for them, and what I hope for you as well, is that we create a life—what we do in it, how we live it—based on purpose. That the things we do in our lives have meaning—meaning to us, not necessarily on any grand scale. What I want most for my children and what I want most for you is a life fulfilled. That your days are meaningful and that your experiences are special. Sometimes we can get a little off track, thinking that cleaning house on the inside and taking control over our lives and our overall health require us to go write a book about it, sing the songs, or get up on a stage. Those are all wonderful things to do, and if you find yourself wishing for any of that, then by all means, go after it with gusto! I will celebrate all your attempts! I just don't want anyone to feel like they have to do anything like that if it's not calling them. Whatever you want to do with your life is up to you. Just don't waste your life. Wasting is done by taking yourself and your life for granted. Wasting is pursuing goals and then dropping out at the last mile. Do not be afraid to be successful. Success is defined by you, not by numbers decided by someone else. Be willing to decide what success means to you, and then create the path to make it come to life. To me, success is not about money, weight, status, fame, or sales numbers. Success to me is being able to say yes to these questions: Did I make a difference? Did I raise strong children who believe in themselves? Did I practice kindness to strangers and loved ones alike? Did I save animals? *Did I make a difference?* is my return statement, no matter what the situation around it might be. It would be wise for you to have a return statement that defines your own success. This will help you create and behave according to your own design.

One last offering: Please always keep gratitude as a front-seat driver. I want you to be able to own the work that you have done to create a more desirable living condition within yourself and relish it. Learning to love yourself can unleash an incredible ripple effect in your life, and that is totally on purpose! Living an extraordinary life doesn't require anything outside yourself. You restore the inside, and the rest will take care of itself. That is something I am certain of. People close to you will likely be triggered by your new internal success. That is on them and has absolutely nothing to do with you. You keep your chin up and your eyes on the prize, putting one strong foot in front of the other. Do your best not to be overly concerned with what other people think of you and try to throw your way. You just keep doing you. That is all anyone needs to ask of themselves.

After all this work of learning how to listen to your body and work with your body for your greatest good and highest joy, it is time now to be set free. I release you out into the world with the hope and wonder of what you will do next. You, my friend, are a superstar, and you can do or be anything you set your heart and mind to do. Just make sure whatever it is, you intended to do it. Be present in your life experiences and focus on what gives meaning to your actions and behaviors. I leave you now with the same three questions that began this book and wonder how different your answers will be:

1 Who are you? Now, who are you, really? What do you stand for now?

____

2 What do you really want? Be specific.

____

3 What are you willing to do to get it?

____

Define your return statement that encompasses your idea of success:

____

____

Final Affirmation:

I am safe.

I am healthy.

I am healed.

I am whole.

I am loved.

I pray you never forget these simple truths. Repeat them often. With all the love in my heart, thank you for sharing this journey with me.

References

1. Zimmerman, Patrick. "How Emotions Are Made." *Noldus Information Technology*, May 18, 2020. https://www.noldus.com/blog/how-emotions-are-made

2. "Trauma and the Body: Out of Home Care Toolbox." Accessed May 26, 2020. https://www.oohctoolbox.org.au/trauma-and-body

3. "Trauma." Trauma / SAMHSA-HRSA. Accessed May 26, 2020. https://www.integration.samhsa.gov/clinical-practice/trauma

4. "Trauma." Missouri Department of Mental Health. Accessed May 26, 2020. https://dmh.mo.gov/healthykids/providers/trauma

5. Pai, Anushka, Alina M. Suris, and Carol S. North. "Posttraumatic Stress Disorder in the DSM-5: Controversy, Change, and Conceptual Considerations." *Behavioral Sciences*, February 13, 2017. https://www.ncbi.nlm.nih.gov/pmc/articles/PMC5371751/

6. Harvard Health Publishing. "Understanding the Stress Response." *Harvard Health*. Accessed May 26, 2020. https://www.health.harvard.edu/staying-healthy/understanding-the-stress-response

7. Ray, Alyssa. "Drs. Paul Nassif & Terry Dubrow Face a Potentially Unsolvable Medical Case on Botched." https://www.eonline.com/shows/botched/news/1090418/drs-paul-nassif-terry-dubrow-face-a-potentially-unsolvable-medical-case-on-botched

8. Boccieri, A. "The Crooked Nose." *Acta otorhinolaryngologica Italica: organo ufficiale della Societa italiana di otorinolaringologia e chirurgia cervico-facciale*, June 2013. https://www.ncbi.nlm.nih.gov/pmc/articles/PMC3709523/

9. "Understanding Trauma Capsules." *PTSD Solutions,* January 13, 2018. https://www.ptsd-trauma.co.uk/understanding-trauma-capsules/

10. "Post-Traumatic Growth." *Trauma Recovery*. Accessed May 26, 2020. https://trauma-recovery.ca/resiliency/post-traumatic-growth/

11. "Kintsugi: The Art of Precious Scars." *LifeGate*, March 27, 2018. https://www.lifegate.com/people/lifestyle/kintsugi

12. "What's in an Acupressure Point? CV8 Spirit Gate..." *Soul Wellness with Melissa Farrugia*, March 27, 2018. http://soulwellness.com.au/kinesiology/acupressure-point-cv8-spirit-gate

13. "BaiHui & Fengchi—Top Points at the Top of the Body." *Acupuncture.com*, November 2008. Accessed May 26, 2020. http://www.acupuncture.com/newsletters/m_nov08/baihui%20fengchi.htm

14. Louie, Dexter, Karolina Brook, and Elizabeth Frates. "The Laughter Prescription: A Tool for Lifestyle Medicine." *American Journal of Lifestyle Medicine*, June 23, 2016. https://www.ncbi.nlm.nih.gov/pmc/articles/PMC6125057/

15. Irimia, R., and M. Gottschling, "Taxonomic Revision of Rochefortia Sw. (Ehretiaceae, Boraginales). Biodiversity Data Journal 4," n.d. https://www.healthline.com/health/what-are-tears-made-of#types

16. Stromberg, Joseph. "The Microscopic Structures of Dried Human Tears." *Smithsonian Institution,* November 19, 2013. https://www.smithsonianmag.com/science-naturethe-microscopic-structures-of-dried-human-tears-180947766/

17. "The Problem with Yelling." NAMI. Accessed May 26, 2020. https://www.nami.org/Blogs/NAMI-Blog/February-2018/The-Problem-with-Yelling

18. "What Happens to a Person's Brain When They Yell?" *Quora*. Accessed May 26, 2020. https://www.quora.com/What-happens-to-a-persons-brain-when-they-yell

19. Harvard Health Publishing. "Understanding the Stress Response." *Harvard Health*. Accessed May 26, 2020. https://www.health.harvard.edu/staying-healthy/understanding-the-stress-response

20. Talley, Nicholas. "Stomach and Mood Disorders: How Your Gut May Be Playing with Your Mind." *The Conversation*, March 2, 2020. https://theconversation.com/stomach-and-mood-disorders-how-your-gut-may-be-playing-with-your-mind-50847

21. Duignan, Brian. "Gaslighting." *Encyclopedia Britannica*, January 13, 2019. https://www.britannica.com/topic/gaslighting

22. "The Basics of Astrocartography." *AstrologyAnswers.com*. Accessed May 26, 2020.

https://astrologyanswers.com/article/the-basics-of-astrocartography/

23. "What Does Healing Mean?" *Definitions*. Accessed May 26, 2020. https://www.definitions.net/definition/Healing

24. "Eye Movements Take Edge Off Traumatic Memories." *ScienceDaily*, September 7, 2018. https://www.sciencedaily.com/releases/2018/09/180907110527.htm

25. Madan, Christopher R., Sarah Scott, and Elizabeth Kensinger. "Positive Emotion Enhances Association-Memory." *ResearchGate*, 2018. https://www.researchgate.net/publication/324819314_Positive_Emotion_Enhances _Association-Memory

26. "Psychology and Smell." *Fifth Sense*. Accessed May 26, 2020. https://www.fifthsense.org.uk/psychology-and-smell/

27. McKennel, S. R., N. M. Withey Barrow, N. M. Bradburn, et al. "The Analysis and Measurement of Happiness as a Sense of Well-Being." *Social Indicators Research*, January 1, 1980.

28. Buckner, Clark. "4 Chemicals That Activate Happiness, and How to Use Them." *TechnologyAdvice*, August 28, 2019. https://technologyadvice.com/blog/information-technology/activate-chemicals-gamify-happiness-nicole-lazzaro/

29. Berrington, Katie, Hayley Maitland, and Alice Newbold. "Katie Berrington." *British Vogue*, March 22, 2016. https://www.vogue.co.uk/gallery/legally-blonde-elle-woods-best-quotes?image=5d545b99c877eb000809830d

30. "Does It Take More Muscles to Frown or Smile?" *Science Made Simple*, March 14, 2020. http://www.sciencemadesimple.co.uk/curriculum-blogs/biology-blogs/muscles

31. Cross, Marie P., Liana Gheorma, and Sarah D. Pressman. "Contrasting Experimentally Device-Manipulated and Device-Free Smiles." *Frontiers in Psychology*, October 15, 2019. https://www.ncbi.nlm.nih.gov/pmc/articles/PMC6803527/

32. Fearnley, Rachel. "Joy vs Happiness." *Psychologies*, September 1, 2015. https://www.psychologies.co.uk/joy-vs-happiness

About the Author

Emily A. Francis is the host of the internet radio show *All About Healing* on Healthy Life Radio. She has a bachelor's degree in exercise science and wellness as well as a master of science in physical education with a concentration in human performance. She graduated from the Atlanta School of Massage in clinical and neuromuscular massage therapy and went on to specialize through the Dr. Vodder School North America in manual lymphatic drainage and combined decongestive therapy working specifically with lymphedema, a chronic condition most notably resulting from effects of cancer treatment. She is a Usui & Karuna Ki Reiki master-level practitioner.

Emily is the author of the books *Stretch Therapy: A Comprehensive Guide to Individual and Assisted Stretching* (Blue River Press, 2013); *Witchy Mama: Magickal Traditions, Motherly Insights & Sacred Knowledge* (Llewellyn Worldwide, 2016); *The Body Heals Itself: How Deeper Awareness of Your Muscles and Their Emotional Connection Can Help You Heal* (Llewellyn Worldwide, 2017); and *Whole Body Healing: Create Your Own Path to Physical, Emotional, Energetic, and Spiritual Wellness* (Llewellyn Worldwide, 2020).

Emily recently made a giant leap from Atlanta, Georgia, and is now living her best life on the island of Malta. To follow her journey, go to www.mymaltalife.com.

You can contact Emily at www.emilyafrancisbooks.com.

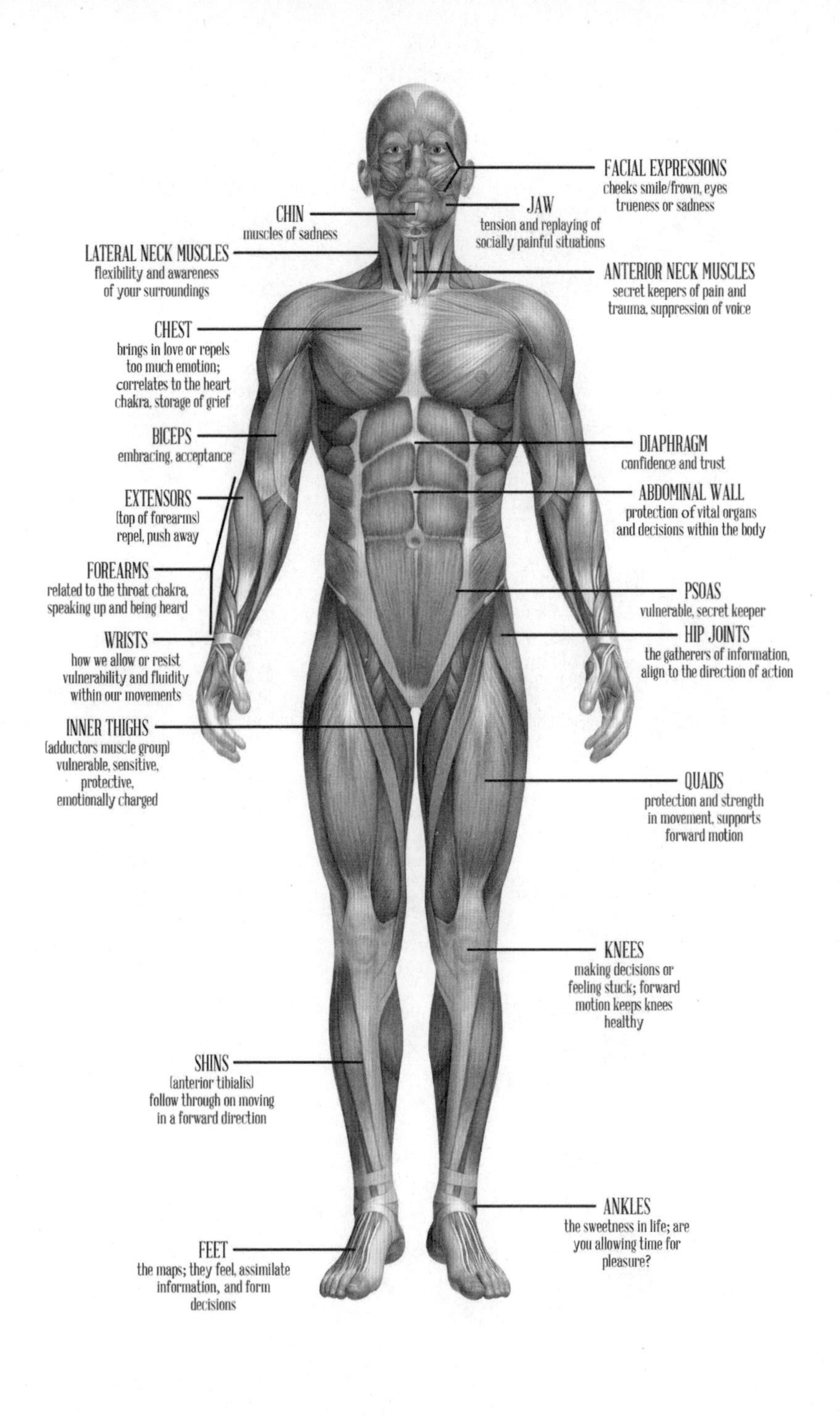
FACIAL EXPRESSIONS
cheeks smile/frown, eyes trueness or sadness
CHIN
muscles of sadness
JAW
tension and replaying of socially painful situations
LATERAL NECK MUSCLES
flexibility and awareness of your surroundings
ANTERIOR NECK MUSCLES
secret keepers of pain and trauma, suppression of voice
CHEST
brings in love or repels too much emotion; correlates to the heart chakra, storage of grief
BICEPS
embracing, acceptance
DIAPHRAGM
confidence and trust
EXTENSORS
(top of forearms) repel, push away
ABDOMINAL WALL
protection of vital organs and decisions within the body
FOREARMS
related to the throat chakra, speaking up and being heard
PSOAS
vulnerable, secret keeper
WRISTS
how we allow or resist vulnerability and fluidity within our movements
HIP JOINTS
the gatherers of information, align to the direction of action
INNER THIGHS
(adductors muscle group) vulnerable, sensitive, protective, emotionally charged
QUADS
protection and strength in movement, supports forward motion
KNEES
making decisions or feeling stuck; forward motion keeps knees healthy
SHINS
(anterior tibialis) follow through on moving in a forward direction
ANKLES
the sweetness in life; are you allowing time for pleasure?
FEET
the maps; they feel, assimilate information, and form decisions

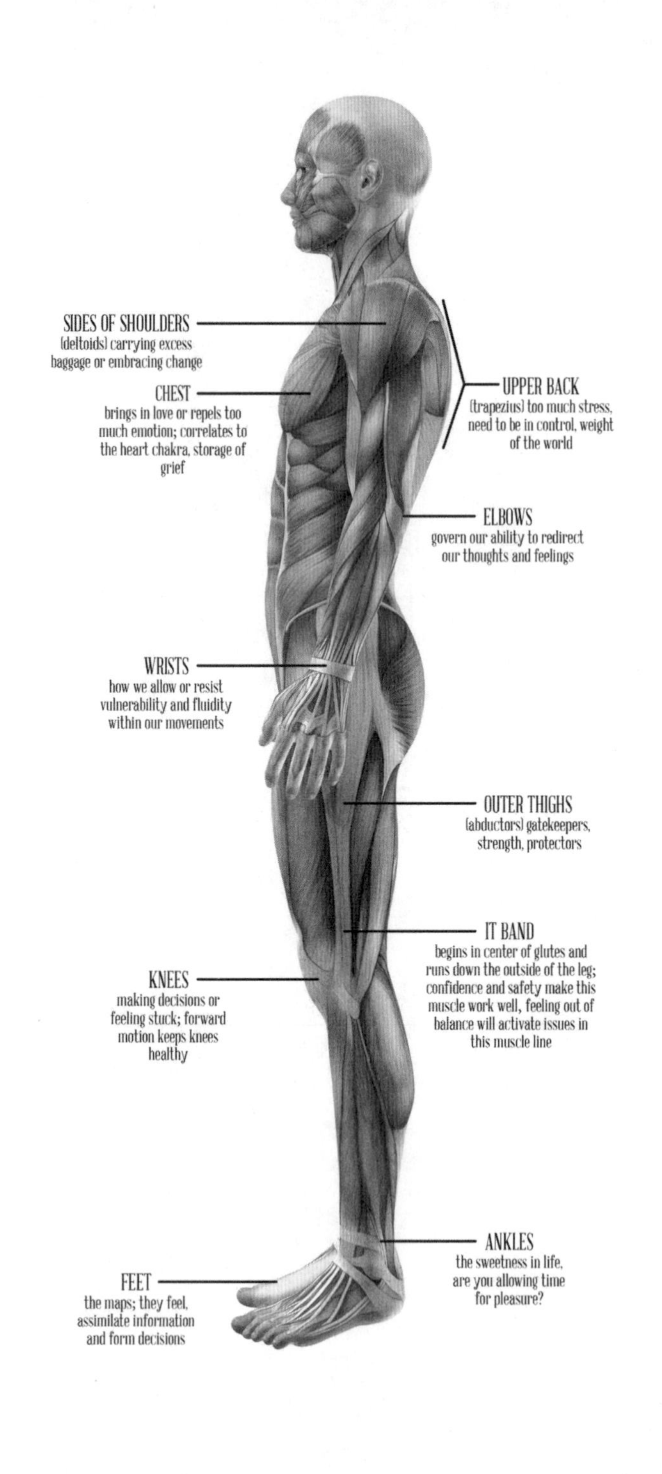
SIDES OF SHOULDERS
(deltoids) carrying excess baggage or embracing change
CHEST
brings in love or repels too much emotion; correlates to the heart chakra, storage of grief
UPPER BACK
(trapezius) too much stress, need to be in control, weight of the world
ELBOWS
govern our ability to redirect our thoughts and feelings
WRISTS
how we allow or resist vulnerability and fluidity within our movements
OUTER THIGHS
(abductors) gatekeepers, strength, protectors
IT BAND
begins in center of glutes and runs down the outside of the leg; confidence and safety make this muscle work well, feeling out of balance will activate issues in this muscle line
KNEES
making decisions or feeling stuck; forward motion keeps knees healthy
ANKLES
the sweetness in life, are you allowing time for pleasure?
FEET
the maps; they feel, assimilate information and form decisions

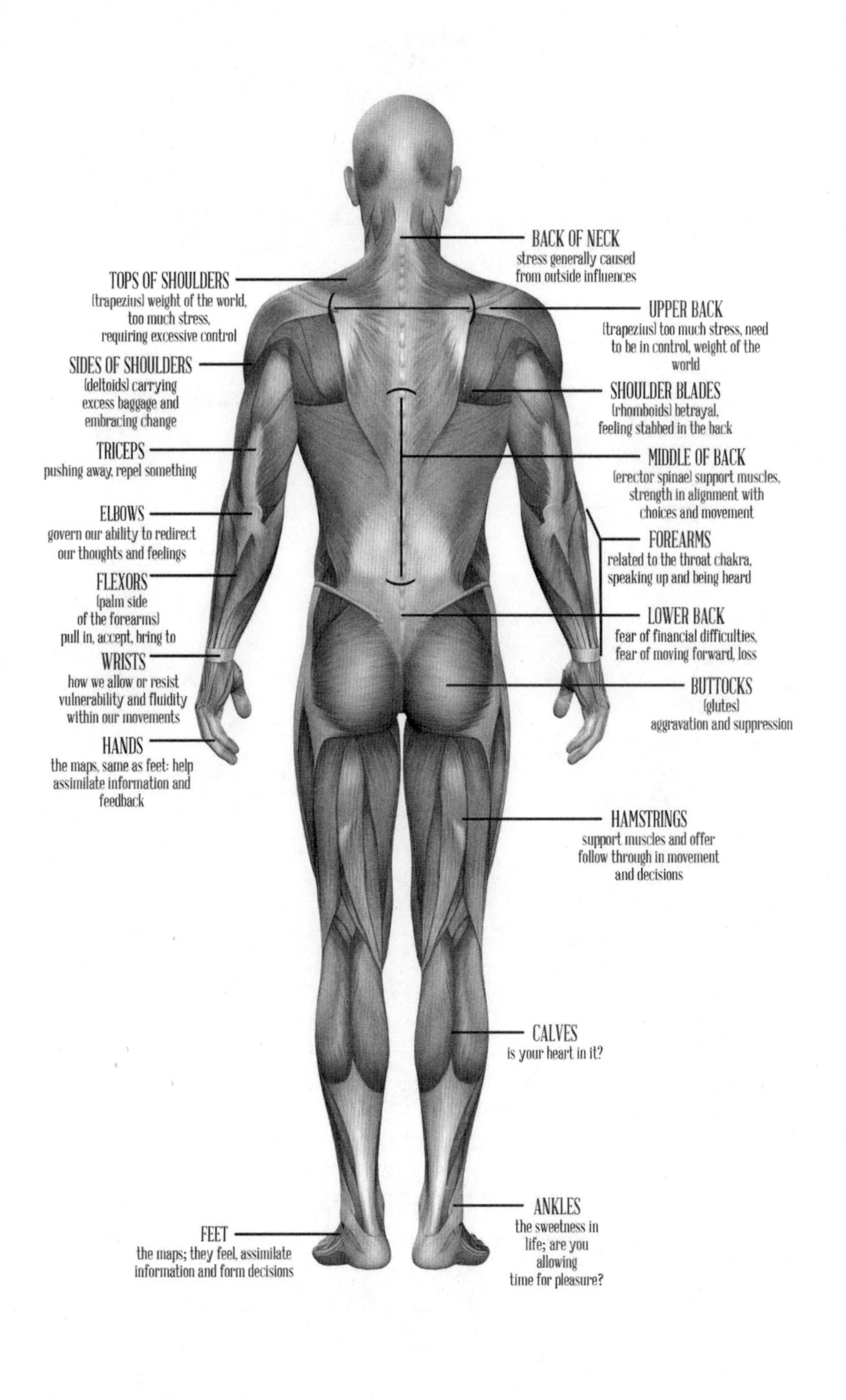
BACK OF NECK
stress generally caused from outside influences
TOPS OF SHOULDERS
(trapezius) weight of the world, too much stress, requiring excessive control
UPPER BACK
(trapezius) too much stress, need to be in control, weight of the world
SIDES OF SHOULDERS
(deltoids) carrying excess baggage and embracing change
SHOULDER BLADES
(rhomboids) betrayal, feeling stabbed in the back
TRICEPS
pushing away, repel something
MIDDLE OF BACK
(erector spinae) support muscles, strength in alignment with choices and movement
ELBOWS
govern our ability to redirect our thoughts and feelings
FOREARMS
related to the throat chakra, speaking up and being heard
FLEXORS
(palm side of the forearms) pull in, accept, bring to
LOWER BACK
fear of financial difficulties, fear of moving forward, loss
WRISTS
how we allow or resist vulnerability and fluidity within our movements
BUTTOCKS
(glutes) aggravation and suppression
HANDS
the maps, same as feet: help assimilate information and feedback
HAMSTRINGS
support muscles and offer follow through in movement and decisions
CALVES
is your heart in it?
ANKLES
the sweetness in life; are you allowing time for pleasure?
FEET
the maps; they feel, assimilate information and form decisions

Notes